SEAN SCULLY
THE CATHERINE PAINTINGS

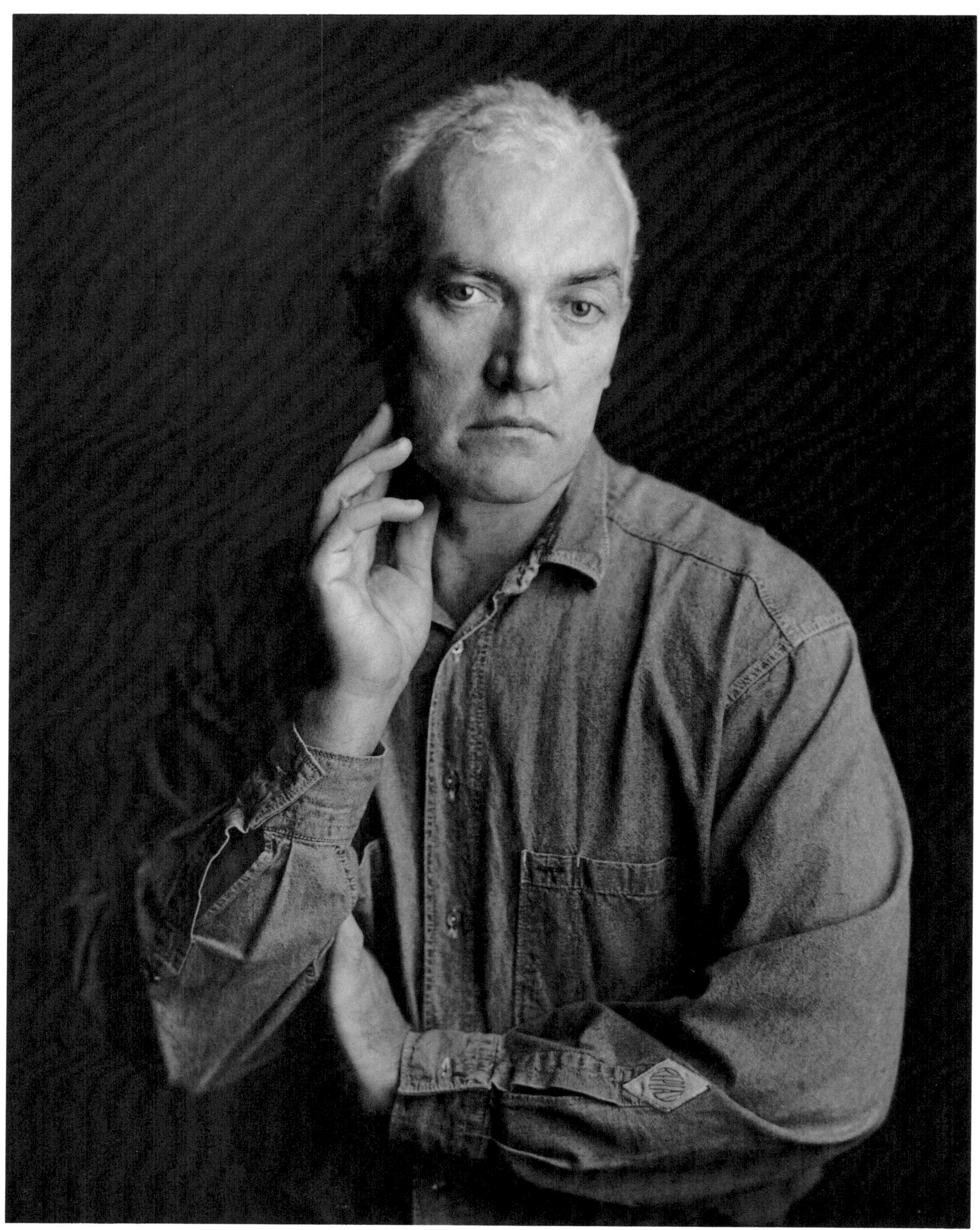

Portrait of Sean Scully by Timothy Greenfield-Sanders ,1992

SEAN SCULLY
THE CATHERINE PAINTINGS

ESSAYS BY
CARTER RATCLIFF
ARTHUR C. DANTO
STEVEN HENRY MADOFF

MODERN ART MUSEUM OF FORT WORTH
1993

Published by the Modern Art Museum of Fort Worth
on the occasion of the exhibition *Sean Scully: The Catherine Paintings*,
May 16—July 25, 1993.

"Sean Scully: The Constitutive Stripe," © 1993, Carter Ratcliff; "Sean Scully's
Catherine Paintings: The Aesthetics of Sequence," © 1993, Arthur C. Danto;
"Wholeness, Partness, and the Gift," © 1993, Steven Henry Madoff. Printed
with permission, all rights reserved.
Photography: Paintings by Sean Scully, pages 8, 10, 11, 12, 13, 14, 22, 27, 31, Fred Scruten, New
York; watercolors by Sean Scully, pages 87-100, Michael Bodycomb, Fort Worth. All works © Sean
Scully, reproduced with permission.
Pages 15, 17, 35, National Gallery of Art, Washington, D. C; page 33, Bonnefantenmuseum,
Maastrict, The Netherlands; pages 37, 43 ; pages 39, 41, 44, Dedalus Foundation, New York.

Cover: Detail, *Catherine*, 1982, by Sean Scully (illustrated page 63).

ISBN: 0-929865-09-X

CONTENTS

FOREWORD

This exhibition of fourteen paintings and thirty-two watercolors by Sean Scully is a very special exhibition.   For the past fourteen years, Scully has chosen a painting that he felt was particularly important or typical of his work of that year, and titled it in honor of his wife, artist Catherine Lee, then retaining that painting for his personal collection. The paintings, one dating from each year from 1979 through 1992, thus offer a small retrospective of the achievement of one of the most important artists at work today. This selection has a more personal importance, however, for the paintings represent Sean Scully's retrospective view of his own work. The group of watercolors included in the exhibition also offer a fascinating study of the artist's working methods. Intended not as studies for the paintings, they reveal the working process by which Scully explores composition and color in a medium of which he is a master.

Both groups of works are exhibited here for the first time, and it is a very great privilege for the Modern Art Museum of Fort Worth to present this exhibition. I would like to express deepest gratitude to Sean Scully and Catherine Lee for their enthusiasm and support of the project, and for their generosity in making these works available. Very special thanks are also due to Per Haubro Jensen for his assistance with all phases of the exhibition's organization.

I would also like to thank the distinguished authors of the essays which follow—Carter Ratcliff, Arthur C. Danto, and Steven Henry Madoff—for their insights into Scully's work in general, and the *Catherine* paintings in particular.

At the Modern Art Museum, a number of individuals have contributed to the realization of this project. Andrea Karnes has provided research and administrative assistance for both the exhibition and catalogue. Rachael Blackburn Wright, registrar, has overseen the assembly and transport of the works in the exhibition. The installation has been directed by Anthony Wright, assisted by Bill LeSueur. The complex task of producing this publication has been managed by Jim Colegrove, with design assistance from Greg Draper. Susan Colegrove has provided administrative assistance throughout all phases of the project.

Scully's 1988 painting, *Pale Fire*, is one of our most important recent acquisitions for the permanent collection of the Modern Art Museum. It is a great honor to be able to present a broader view of this important artist's work through the beautiful paintings in this exhibition.

Marla Price
Director

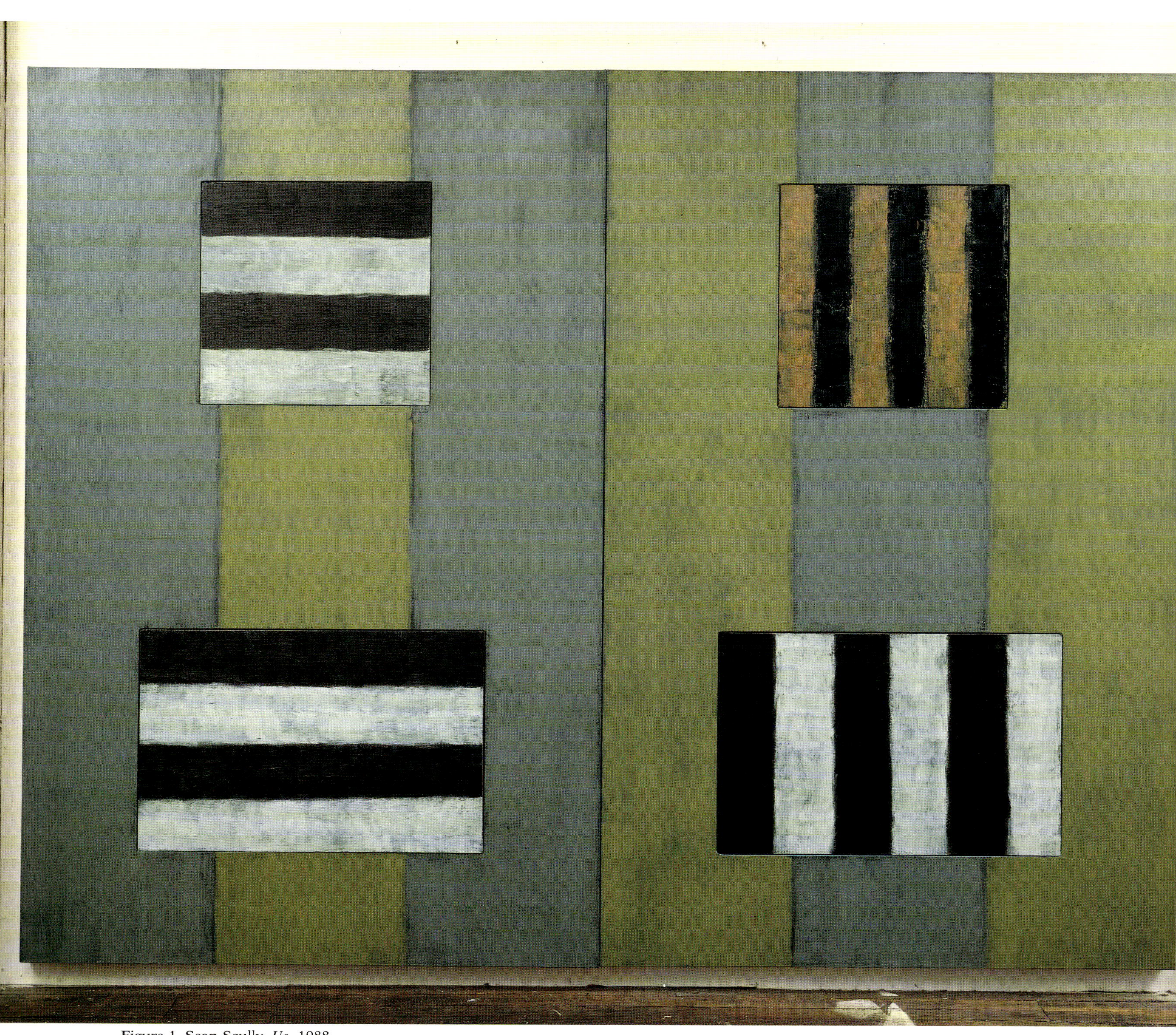

Figure 1. Sean Scully, *Us*, 1988
Oil on canvas, 96 x 120 inches.

Sean Scully: The Constitutive Stripe
by Carter Ratcliff

A few years ago Sean Scully told an audience in Berkeley, California, that "the subject in my paintings is the way the stripe is painted, and that is no different to me than Cezanne's apple or his bottle, which he painted over and over again. The stripe is neutral and boring—you see it all over the place—and that makes the stripe receptive to interpretation." [1] Scully interprets it as an endlessly adaptable block for building the "large structures that are what represent us and our culture for all time," as he said in a recent conversation. "You see these structures first in Cimabue, Giotto, Masaccio. Then the structures disappear. The tradition is broken as Michelangelo and Caravaggio get interested in the space around figures. The Baroque is a matter of theater. But the mainstream never disappears completely. Artists continue to give expression to the large structures, trying to get to the heart of them." [2] Scully has been trying for nearly 20 years.

At first he worked on canvases in the standard format: four corners, one surface. Since the early 1980s, he has assembled his pictures from at least two panels, often more, and in 1987 he set a small canvas into a large one. There were more insets, sometimes as many as four to a painting. Recently they vanished but not, I think, for good. Whatever structural part it plays, a panel always bears stripes laid on in two alternating colors. *White Window* (1988) (Fig.2) presents an exception: an inset panel, the "window" of the title, with six

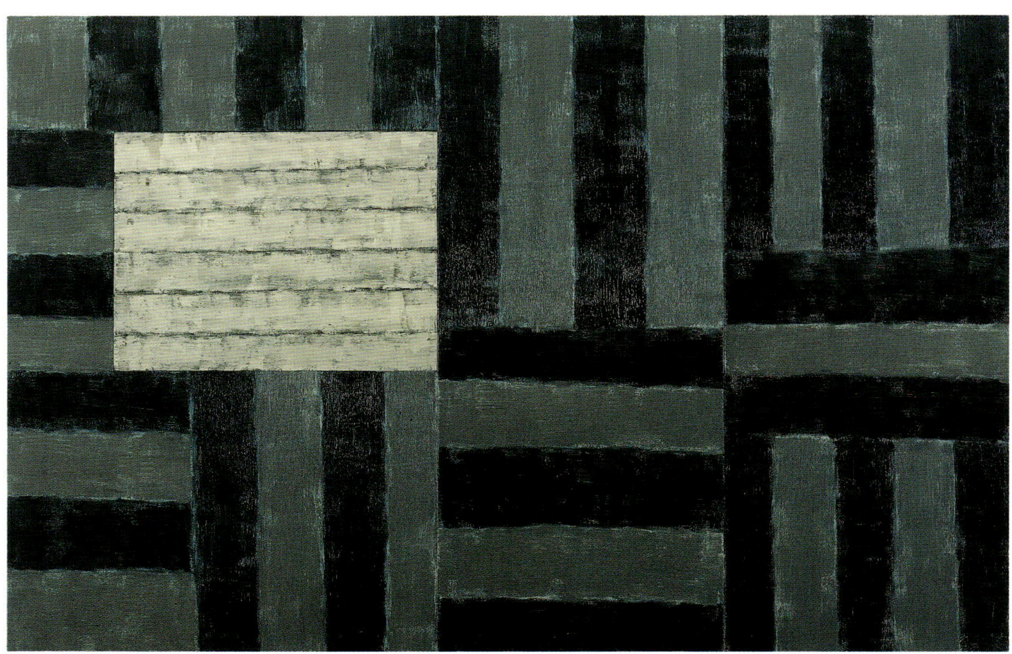

Figure 2. Sean Scully, *White Window*, 1988
Oil on canvas, 96 x 146 inches.

horizontal stripes, all white. Elsewhere, small panels contain one wide stripe. Or that is how I interpret the solidly monochrome surfaces in a picture like *All There Is* (1986), (Fig. 3) for nothing in Scully's oeuvre should be explained without reference to stripes.

He begins a picture with a quick preparatory notation, less a drawing than a rough diagram. Painting a panel, Scully improvises its exact shade and sometimes the number of its stripes. Then, on a wall of his New York studio, he tries finished panels in various configurations before settling on the one that will constitute a new work. All is provisional until everything clicks. At the start of his career, he applied stripes in strict accordance with preset plans, and his brushwork was rigidly impersonal. As the 1980s began, he taught his hand to relax. Applying oil paints wet-on-wet, he let his stripes widen and come alive with nuance. Earlier, pictures had soaked up real light with blotter-like efficiency. That absorbency is gone. His recent pictures seem to generate light slowly, from the underlayers of color you see here and there through the brusque and ruminative textures of the surface.

Sometimes the paint is thick enough to warp the canvas. This warpage is local and slight, an effect far from sculptural. Yet it inclines the eye to read his patterns of stripes as arrangements of substantial things: large bricks or beams or squared-away stones. Scully admires modernist architects like Le Corbusier and Mies van der Rohe, though he has none of their puritanical restraint. The colors of his pigments are lush in a somber way, and they spread sensuously over the canvas. His affinity for the severities of 20th-century form-givers like Corbu shows when he places broad stripes in post-and-lintel patterns. These arrange-

10

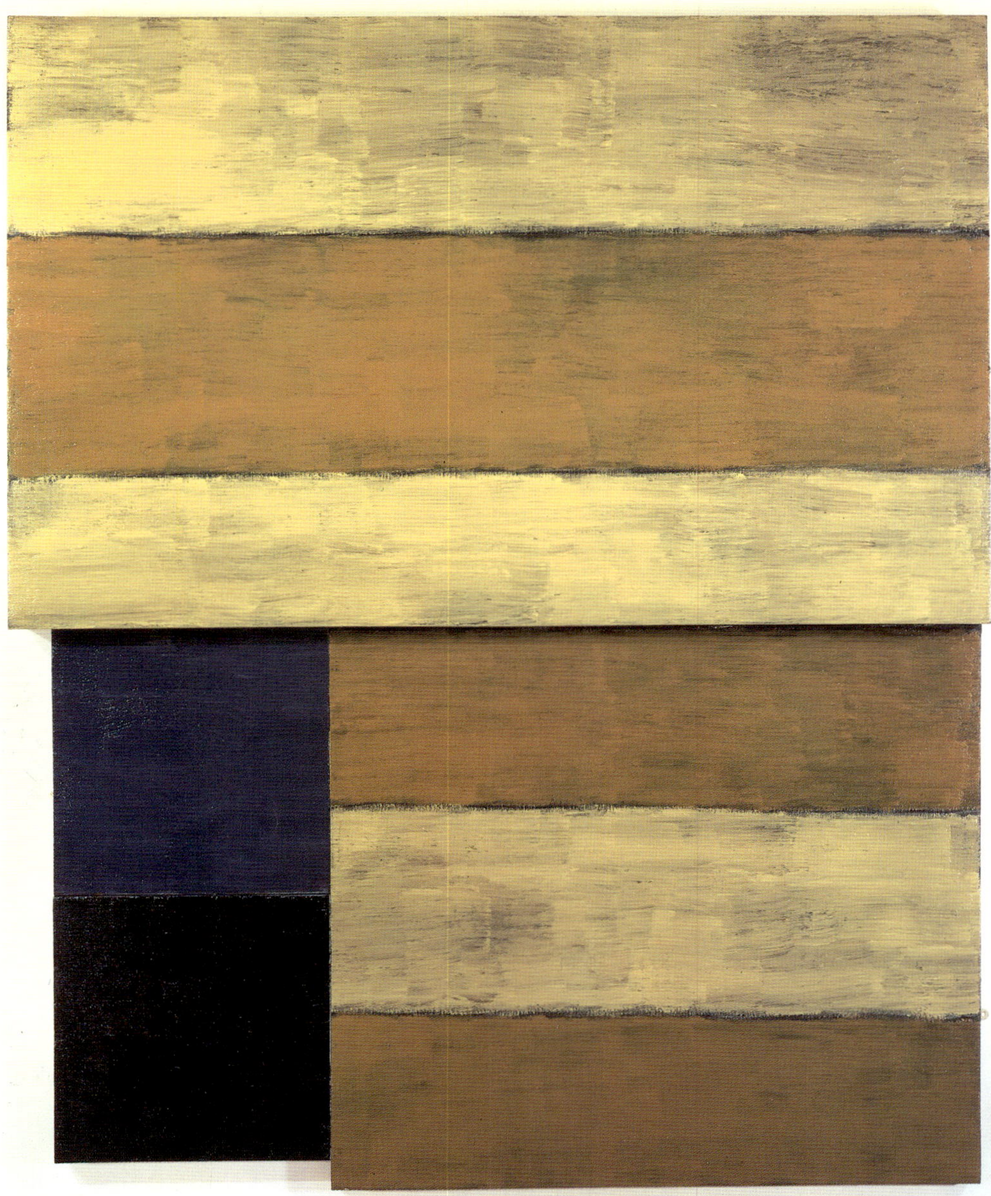

Figure 3. Sean Scully, *All there is*, 1986
Oil on canvas, 106 x 84 inches.

ments also recall Stonehenge and the houses children make of wooden blocks.
White stripes alternating with black ones in *Stare* (1984) (Fig. 4) refer obliquely
to old half-timbered houses, or so it seems to me. Unlike hard-line modernists of
earlier generations, Scully does nothing to discourage idiosyncratic speculation.
If his paintings remind you of buildings or light or weather, if they stir speculations about political order at the end of the second millennium, that is all right
with him.

His canvases get their look of architecture from our willingness to see
their patterns as squared-away—as they are, but not precisely. With skewed
corners and edges out of plumb, Scully's stripes picture the irregularities visited

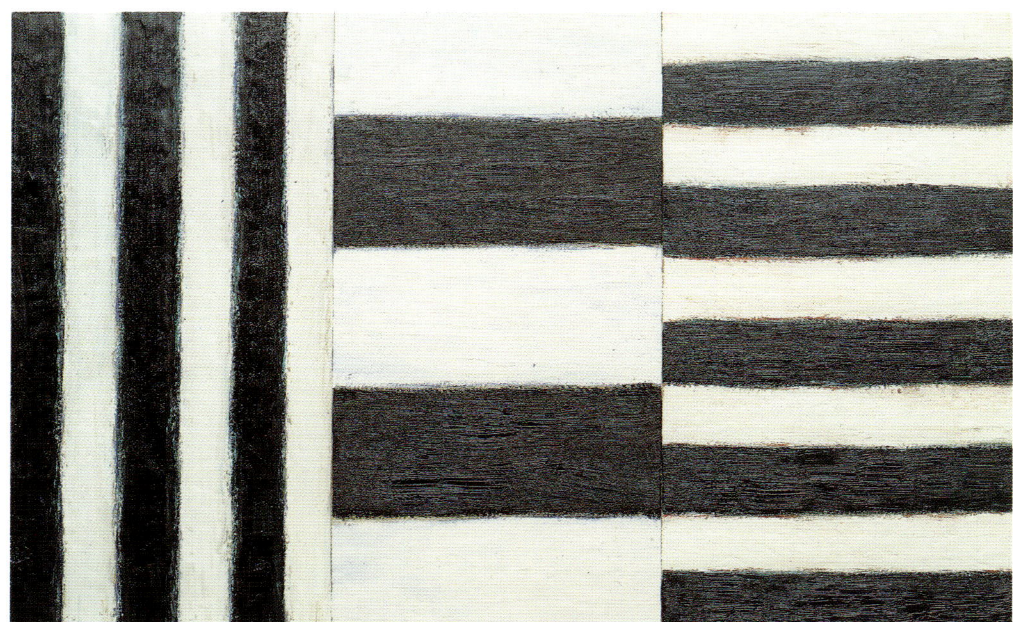

Figure 4. Sean Scully, *Stare*, 1984
Oil on canvas, 38 x 60 inches.

over the seasons on forms built to be strictly rectilinear: the more ancient the beam, the more eccentric its shape. Up close, departures from strict geometric order look more textural than structural, and they work in a different way. Now, instead of picturing the effects of time and weight on joints and beams, they show the blunt, sometimes willful tone of the painter's gestures. Scully doesn't like to give his own premises total obedience: against a pattern's rigid dictates, the hand rebels.

Then, when you look at a painting from a distance, it alludes to buildings in clusters and to bird's-eye view of cultivated terrain. The luminosity of his color strengthens, and you feel the force of the weather. In the black and white regions of *Red Ascending* (1990), (Fig. 5) the light is bleak but intense, as if angled off patches of ice. The red zone of this painting generates a velvety glow, seductive by virtue of its seeming self-absorption. This inwardness has no miniaturizing effect. Like his other pictures, *Red Ascending* seems vast because the artist leaves it wide open to surmise. Each variant of his light establishes a climate. I feel a cold brilliance in *Black Garden* (1990). The atmosphere of *City of Dreams* (1989) (Fig. 6) feels dense and warm to me.

Scully's weather engenders emotional tones too subtle to name, and it is always tempting to exchange his complexities for simplicities. Giving in to this temptation, I let signs of his gesture drift to the margins of my attention, taking with them the artist's allusions to buildings and landscapes. I note the way his painted stripes echo the edges of his stretchers, showing his respect for a modernist ideal: the painting that renders itself pure by ignoring everything but itself. By now, an effect of formal purity is filling the image. Yet this effect of purity is not purity itself. It is another of Scully's allusions, his reference to the purely

12

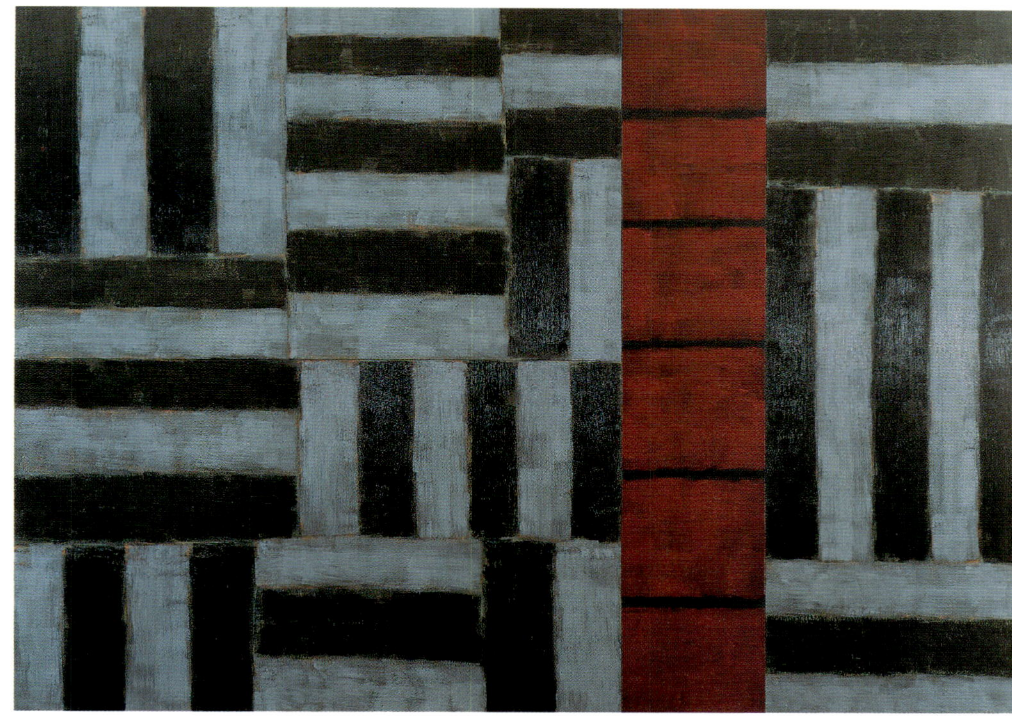

Figure 5. Sean Scully, *Red Ascending*, 1990
Oil on canvas, 102 x 140 inches

pictorial picture, a modernist ideal that his history won't let him deny. Among
the predecessors he has chosen are Bridget Riley, Francois Morellet, and other
painters who embraced this ideal. They believe in it, as Scully cannot. He is an
ironic purist, an abstract painter who learned in the act of painting that there is
no such thing as abstraction—not, at least, in any strong sense of the word. Yet
he honors the ideal of pure art, as he rejects the hope of it. This double gesture
launches the subtleties of his art.

*

Scully was born in Dublin, in 1945. Four years later, he moved with his
family to London, and, at the age of 20, entered that city's Croydon College of
Art. Continuing at Newcastle University, in the north of England, his education
as a painter ended in 1973 with the completion of a Harvard fellowship. Two
years later, Scully settled in the United States. "I was still at Newcastle," Scully
remembers, "when I understood that Mark Rothko and Jackson Pollock had
found a new way to put things together—an American way. The energy runs
right off the edges of the canvas. I wanted that openness, but I also wanted the
plastic clarity of Mondrian." I think there was more that he wanted from Piet
Mondrian and those who joined him under the banner of de Stijl.

With results that continue to influence art and design, de Stijl's brand of
geometric abstraction subordinated small forms to large, according to the dictates of balanced composition or "dynamic equilibrium," as Mondrian called it.
Historians customarily say that he arrived at the elements of his style—his white
field, black stripes, and rectangles of red, yellow, and blue—by reducing his

13

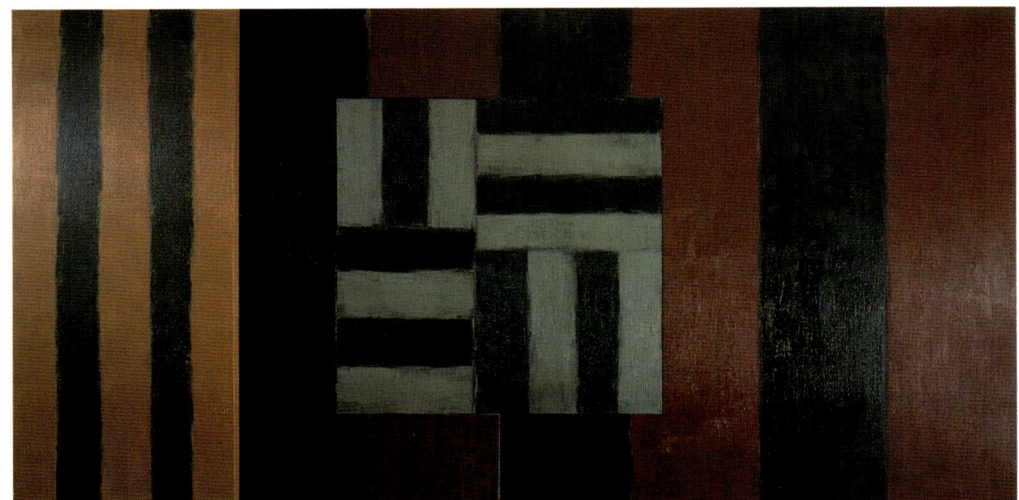

Figure 6. Sean Scully, *City of Dreams*, 1989
Oil on canvas, 96 x 186 inches.

pictorial means. He did, but this account advances the misleading notion that Mondrian was a pure painter who excluded from the picture everything not pictorial. His art is not exclusionary. With utopian fervor, he rendered his imagery general enough to allude to, and thus include, everything.

Like many other European avant-gardists, Mondrian believed that modern societies twist modern selves into awkward, nonfunctional shapes, or it shatters them. He proposed art as a force in the struggle to reassemble the self and reconcile it to society. First, art would have to become orderly. As painting advanced toward perfection, it would abandon itself. It would become sculpture. Sculpture would become architecture, architecture would become urban design. As small units of form assumed their places in large compositions, so the citizens of the future's perfected city would be subsumed by large and well-organized social structures. To fulfill their individuality, individuals would undergo a vaguely Hegelian process of integration with spiritual forces not merely symbol-ized but bodied forth by visual form correctly harmonized. Thus would egos transcend the destructive impulses of egoism. History, if it persisted in de Stijl's utopia, would be incapable of producing horrors like First World War, which had driven Mondrian and his geometric colleagues to their apocalyptic faith in the powers of composition.

Leon Battista Alberti, the first major theorist of Renaissance form, considered it "well to know what composition is in painting. I say composition is that rule in painting by which the parts fit together in the painted work." He adds that only if the work displays "variety" will it give pleasure. [3] But how do we know if the parts of an image make an orderly fit, or if their way of fitting bal-ances the demand for order against the need to inflect that order with variety? We must decide each case on its merits, for, as David Hume wrote, "It is allowed on all hands that beauty, as well as virtue, always lies in a medium; but where this medium is placed, is the great question, and can never be sufficiently ex-

14

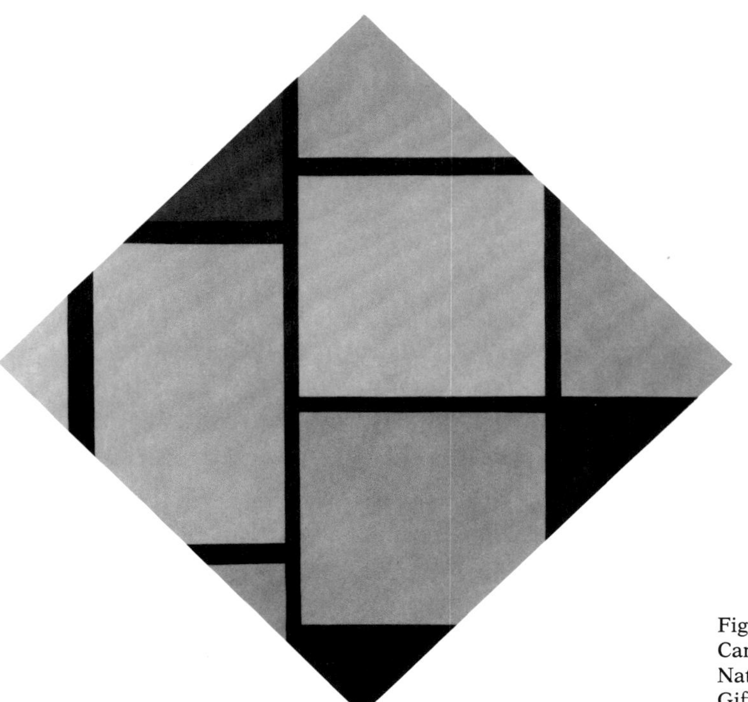

Figure 8. Piet Mondrian, *Diamond Painting in Red, Yellow, and Blue*, c. 1921/1925
Canvas on hardboard, diamond 56 ¼ x 56 inches (1.428 x 1.423 cm.)
National Gallery of Art, Washington,
Gift of Herbert and Nannette Rothschild

plained by general reasonings." [4]

Mondrian's penchant for "general reasonings" gives his theories of "dynamic equilibrium" a bright, cloudy dazzle that defeats a close reading. Nonetheless, from his paintings and writings one gathers a heroic if not a clear image of Mondrian's ideal artist: a leader qualified to guide everything, including the self, to its point of absorption in a hierarchy of formal, social, and spiritual absolutes. So the degree of selfhood's self-liquidation is the measure of its success. Analogously, individual paintings were to point beyond their individuality to utopian developments in sculpture and architecture. By contrast—and the contrast is sharp—Scully's works present themselves as specific and sufficient in their specificity. They posit the self as the persistent, indispensable presence that gives significance and a local order to accumulations of fragments. Elaborating particulars, encouraging their allusiveness, Scully shows a command of detail more useful now than the flair for transcendental generalization displayed by Mondrian and his colleagues. Yet those artists are among the most important of Scully's esthetic forebears—more important to him than, say, Morellet, whose idea of abstraction's purpose was much narrower. With his mastery of composition, Scully preserves the memory of utopian artists like Mondrian and of the citizen who was to be absorbed—and redeemed—by utopian hierarchies.

*

Scully's patterns of stripes present the eye with rock-solid certainties about the fitness of horizontals to give support to verticals. Just as confidently, verticals buttress horizontals. Varying these arrangements with grand reversals,

15

Scully confirms the certainties he offers. Then, as the eye follows formal variety into niceties of proportion and texture, the authority of composition's monumental order fades. That authority reasserts itself when one steps back from a canvas for a general view. Yet, even at a distance, each of Scully's stripes is too specifically itself to be completely assimilated by the composition. In particularity is strength. Nonetheless, the black and gray stripes of *White Window* (Fig. 2) seem tenuous in comparison to the ghostly white of the inset panel that gives the painting its name. Looked at long enough, this striated monochrome gathers the painting's solidity to itself, leaving the dark stripes in a wraith-like state. Recalling the stripes of an all-white flag by Jasper Johns, the inset has another effect. It brings up the subject of America, that region of Western culture where traditional structures do not always obtain a purchase on form or meaning.

As Scully understood before he left school in England, American painters devised new ways to arrange a picture's parts. Intimating the infinite, the Americans give an arbitrary feel to a canvas's edges, those palpable facts which, in Mondrian's pictures, coincide with compositional boundaries. Mondrian noted that, in principle, composition can be expanded forever. Had de Stijl realized in full its utopian plans, "dynamic equilibrium" would have covered the globe. However, this expansion would have generated a series of linked compositions, each internally coherent and bounded by firm, easily discerned limits. Pictures by Pollock, Barnett Newman, and other New York painters construed the infinite differently, for their pictures include no principle of enclosure. Wide open and utterly indeterminate in scale, they deprive the frame of its containing force. Many British and European artists have recoiled from the peculiarly American openness of the allover image, as it came to be known. Scully did not, for his doubts about transcendent order on the European model made him sympathetic to American paintings and their localized logic, which he has reinvented. Yet he refused to forsake Mondrian, his exemplary master of composition. And Scully had a particular use for Mondrian's stripes, for they showed him "how to geometrize Pollock."

The New York critic Henry McBride spent the 1920s and 30s monitoring American attempts to learn compositional structure from Cubism and, later, from Mondrian and de Stijl. Then, in 1949, he saw one of Pollock's dripped canvases, which he described as a picture of "a flat, war-shattered city, possibly Hiroshima, as seen from a great height in moonlight." Shocked by Pollock's willingness to dispense with compositional order, McBride invoked atomic disaster. [5] To less easily appalled observers, the drip paintings looked like newly discovered territory, zones where something unexpected was emerging. What did emerge is still fresh because so few have thoroughly seen it.

When Pollock turned drawing into paint slinging, he changed the nature of pictorial form. No longer was a line, a shape, or an incident of color an

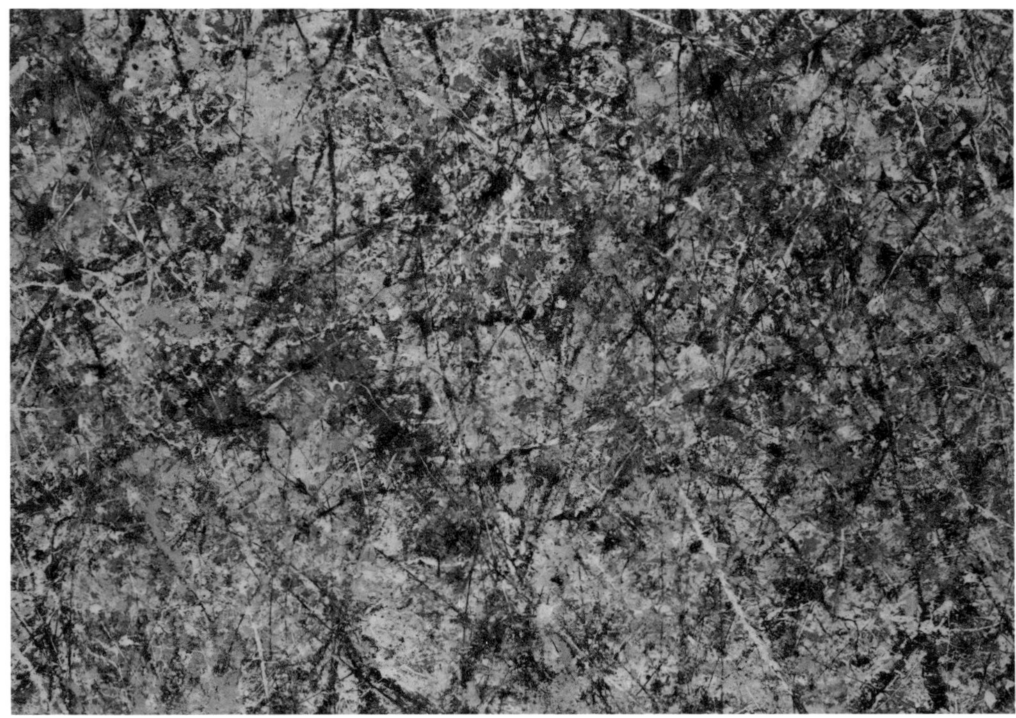

Figure 7. Jackson Pollock, *Number 1, 1950
(Lavender Mist)*, 1950
National Gallery of Art, Washington
Ailsa Mellon Bruce Fund.

element of a large, integrated structure. His method permitted no such structure
to emerge. Unable to serve as part of a whole, each detail of an allover image is
itself a whole, a unit of form sufficient in itself. So a splash or wiry curve of
pigment can exert, at most, a local and tentative authority over other curves and
splashes. It is customary to say that Pollock's dripping is a variant of Surrealist
automatism. It is, though comments like these induce us to zero in on small
issues in the history of technique. His wide, allover tangles of color bear on
America's largest and most elusive ideas about itself.

Dripping and sloshing his pigments, Pollock often (but not always) gave
their textures enough intensity to immerse the eye. Immediacies overwhelm
vision, and when it finds its way to the edge of a canvas this physical limit feels
incidental. According to its own, localized logic, the picture could spread far
beyond the edges to a shape dictated by its own idiosyncracies. Only contingent
details tie a drip painting, in its particularity, to the generality of the canvas—that
familiar, rectangular surface. Pollock's allover images are restless, and the social
implications of their restlessness are vexing. In fitting form to canvas,
Mondrian's best pictures give the results an air of inevitable rightness. Thus they
are emblems of the hope that individuals can be matched, with harmonious ease,
to the demands of a hierarchical society. Because Pollock's pictures offer the
individual no large order to join, it's difficult to give these works a social reading.
In their immensity, they have elbow room for only one individual: the artist who
made them with his large, unencumbered gestures or the viewer who traces the
evidence of those gestures—Pollock's web of slung pigment. The drip paintings

make sense as products of the American impulse to posit oneself as the sole inhabitant of one's ideal world.

This is a flagrantly impractical impulse. Still, it has animated many Americans, even some who paid sophisticated attention to the need for social order and governmental authority. During the 1850s Ralph Waldo Emerson claimed that political turmoil was ushering in the time "when the civil machinery that has been the religion of the world decomposes to dust and smoke before the new adult individualism; and the private man feels that he is the State." [6] In utopian programs like de Stijl's, conflict ceases when egos abandon egoism for a place in a transcendent structure. For Emerson and for those later Americans who painted allover images, the ego avoids conflict by recognizing only itself. So Pollock's drip paintings are illegible as emblems of social order. Their meanings come into focus only when we read in them his will to see the world as a void to be filled with the textures of his being.

I have described this as an American need, though one could point to signs of it in English Romanticism at its most deliriously self-infatuated. Further, it was a horror of European, not American egoism, that led de Stijl to promote the transcendence of the ego. Nonetheless, absolute, asocial egoism found a pictorial reflection only in American painting, as Scully saw—or sensed—when he was a student. After leaving school he tried to reconcile Mondrian and Pollock, composition and noncomposition. His art entered maturity in the early 1980s, when he acknowledged that he couldn't: the two are so incompatible that they can't even oppose each other. Each posits a view that excludes the idea of the other.

Sometimes, as they establish a pattern of checks and balances, Scully's stripes produce a compositional balance as solid as any to be seen in Mondrian's paintings. A moment later, his most thoroughly resolved composition can look like a fragment of a striped, allover field—each fragment infinite in its potential for repetition and in its impatience with boundaries. Refusing to settle on one option at the expense of the other, Scully inflects alloverness with compositional order and disrupts that order with alloverness. This is the behavior of a skeptic unpersuaded by any generalizing ideal and reluctant to promulgate generalizations of his own.

From this reluctance comes the unsettled weather in a Scully painting. Each of its regions is a micro-climate trying to establish itself as the standard for judging the others too hot, too steamy, too dusty, or too satisfied to hover between a dark, dank green and the paradoxical chill of a sharp orange. But no set of stripes makes itself the measure of the rest. When you try to see the basis of this local independence, the eye focuses on details of paint and canvas that show up metaphors of weather and landscape as metaphorical. Their figurative natures exposed, these tropes don't vanish, or even lose their force. Figurative readings persist, no matter how insistent the facts of form and texture may be. Scully provokes a stand off—facts against tropes. There are more elusive tensions between the various rates of time that flow through a picture's several zones and carry the imagination back into the work's weather patterns. These return the eye to painted patterns. Scully encourages no transcendental flights. His monumental ambiguities leave us stranded at ground level before large objects that sometimes look alien in their militant individuality.

*

We are used to the feeling that pop-culture images, and especially on television, are weightless and disposable. Reflexively, we assume that images in art galleries have more substance. Nonetheless, a high-art image can seem as flimsy as a television ad, especially if it is designed to illustrate some esthetic point or carry out a maneuver of style. Much that we see in the galleries is thin, glib, and lightweight. Scully's paintings are weighty, dense, obdurate. They are "about surfaces," he says, adding they are also about

> real time—the hours I actually spend in a particular place in a
> certain light covering a certain surface with precisely the colors
> and shapes and textures you see on that surface. I admire Im-
> pressionism as much for its textures as for the light beyond the
> surface of the paint. Imagery has to stay on the surface, it has to
> be about surface and the way it is painted, if it is going to felt.
> Otherwise, the painter is just presenting an idea about painting.

Scully likes the palpability of paint, so El Greco and Velazquez don't much interest him as masters of "spatial effects." What he likes about their canvases is the way their bear their burdens of color and

> how the surface articulates the large structures that give things
> shape in Western culture. Van Gogh made the breakthrough to
> modern art. The sheer physical urgency of his need to paint broke
> down the pretense of pictorial depths. Everything stays on the
> surface. His structures become tangible. A blind person could
> read his paintings, and of course his subjects are extremely
> moving, sometimes, but his real power is as an abstractionist.
> The real poignancy and power of his art is in the way he worked
> the paint.

Yet Mondrian, Scully's exemplary European, and many postwar New Yorkers permitted no heavy buildup of pigment. Whether they enclosed the canvas in a compositional structure or opened it up, these artists wanted their art to transcend matters of surface and edge.

Newman did not use his stripes—or "zips," as he called them—to measure his glowing reaches of color. With their unanchored self-reliance, the zips argue that these immensities are immeasurable. Like Rothko, Newman intended alloverness to give off a radiance, blazing or subtle, that would discredit mundane facts like the edges of a canvas. Pollock, too, wanted the dark, shifting gleam of his dripped images to render the tangible surface of his canvas insignificant. Like northern landscapists of earlier centuries, these New York painters found the sublime in invocations of light.

Younger New Yorkers let the light dim. Jasper Johns endowed his Stars and Stripes—the Flag paintings of the mid-1950s with a rubbery, encaustic smolder. By the end of the decade, Frank Stella had covered a series of canvases with stripes of tarry, absorptive black. Johns, Stella, and certain Minimalists generated alloverness from arrays of endlessly repeatable modules: stripes, boxes, metal plates. They induced an earlier generation's sublime to descend to earth and become tangible. Scully read in their art signs that New York is the place where surfaces are toughest and bear the greatest weight of meaning. So he came here, and New York's improvised, allover sprawl cued much of the incident in Scully's paintings of this decade.

In New York, Scully did construction work for a time. "You have a job to do—putting up a wall, leaving windows and things—but there is always some leeway," Scully has said in conversation. "I used to indulge myself privately, trying to make the job fun by composing the elements in a satisfying way." In New York streets, Scully attunes his eye to the expedients of building sites. "It's interesting to see how people patch things," he says.

> You can tell from the way a construction worker nails a plywood
> sheet into place that no one is reverent. They simply do what
> works at the moment. Sometimes the metal patches on the
> sidewalk are even rougher. I see a sort of urban romance in the
> makeshifts people use to keep a place like Manhattan together,
> though of course that is the point—it doesn't exactly hold to-
> gether. It's not contained. There's the grid of streets and the
> gridded buildings and then all the amazing things people do
> inside those grids and along their edges.

Imposed by circumstances, form can be inflected. "Driving along the Pacific coast of Mexico," says Scully,

> I've seen squarish houses painted with big patches of blue or red
> or some other color. Bright yellow or blue. Then the blue runs

out and people begin a patch of red. You see totally subjective
responses to the impersonal geometry of a house, and that
redeems it. That's wonderful, like Minimalist painting gone
wrong.

Or Minimalism gone right, rescued from generality. He wants the pictorial to
picture, among other things, its own state of contingency. So each of his pictures
insists on its physical nature, its weight and shape and texture, its existence as an
individual object irreducible to principle or program.

*

Exerting their expansive, allover energies, Scully's stripes lead the eye to
edges, abutments, and more stripes with different textures—details that stress the
presence of canvas and stretcher bars. His panels tempt the touch. At their most
insistent, they advance to become boxy projections. One could see here a revival
of the Minimalist plan to detach paintings from the wall: stretched canvas
becomes sculpture, ambiguous image becomes simple object. The writer Joseph
Masheck has seen more deeply. In an interview with Scully, he said of the
projecting surfaces that

> Although they have a constructional aspect, even a certain archi-
> tectural bravura, these reliefs are "non-load-bearing." They are
> not trading in material masses.
> Scully: I've always been concerned with something Johns did,
> and something that Beckett has done in some of his plays: the
> artist introduces a kind of jolt; what he says is "O.K., this is
> fiction and this isn't fiction." So the fiction is broken all the
> time . . . . That is the reason I do it [make projecting panels]. It
> has nothing to do with the paintings as being overtly physical; I
> think, in fact, they're quite discreet, physically. I could make the
> projections much larger, getting into something else, like Stella;
> but I'm only doing this to break the fiction of the paintings. [7]

Scully begins to break the fiction of the formally correct artwork when he leads
the viewer to ask, for instance, why does this panel and not another advance?
The fiction collapses when the viewer sees that the artist has taken care to
provide not even the illusion of an answer to that question. No play of pictorial
logic gives the impression that he had to extend a certain panel just this far and
no farther. From the trial arrangements that lead to their eventual configurations, his pictures take on a look of contingency. It's as if they remember that
they could be entirely other than they are.

By 1987 Scully was again aligning panels to form a single surface. In

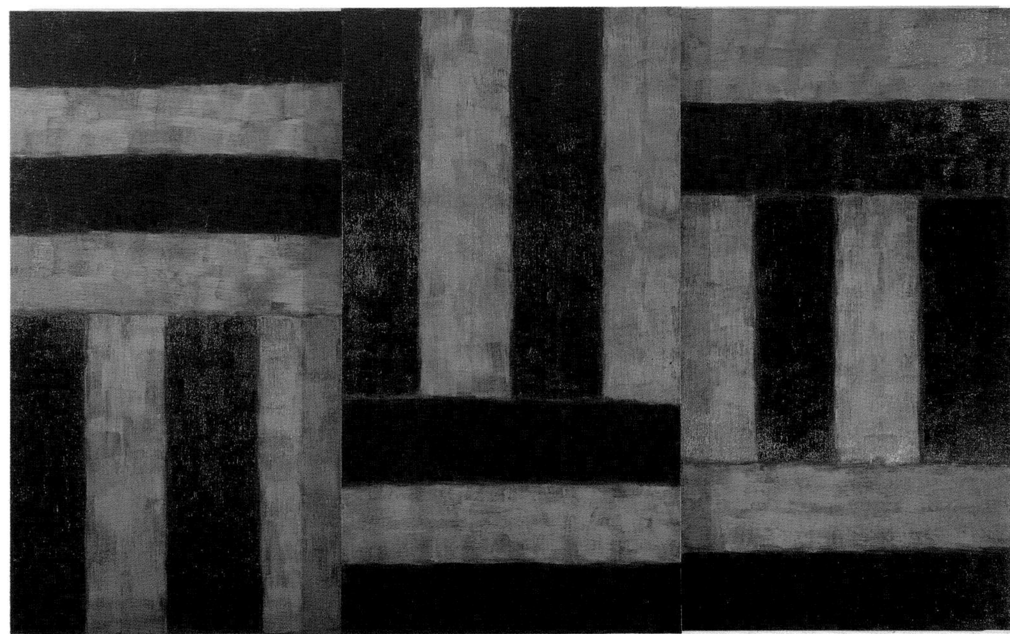

Figure 9. Sean Scully, *Durango*, 1990
Oil on canvas, 114 x 180 inches.

works like *China Seas* (1990) and *Durango* (1990), (Fig. 9) surfaces are again
stepped. Instead of marching forward, Scully appears to be tracing a circle,
though of course things are not so easily understood. The first projections are
aggressive. The latest ones do not look like reprises, for they are easy to miss at
first glance. They are subtle, producing a previously unseen effect of slippage.
Arguing that a carpentered division is more real than a painted one, these new
projections make their point with enough finesse to invite the counter-argument
that in the realm of the pictorial, what is painted is no less substantial than three-
dimensional detail. Or flat, painted form may have greater substance. Eventu-
ally, one sees the new projections as both physically assertive and ghostly. It is
fitting to find this ambiguity in abstractions that, here and there, look realistic,
that are architectonic and contained, yet implicitly boundless. Composed and
not composed, Scully's pictures belong to the tradition of Mondrian. Yet they
evolved from Pollock's allover paintings, which do not so much deny Mondrian
as attain a sublime indifference to him and his speculations about transcendent
order.

*

Looking for the large matters Scully addresses, I thought of the relation
between a code of laws and a written constitution, for it resembles the relation
between figure painting, with its recognizable subject matter, and abstraction,
which has none. Figure painters might object, and I ought to say that what
follows has nothing to do with right and wrong or legality and illegality. However, I do touch on legitimacy, not the moral but the esthetic kind. For I believe
that, as law derives from a written constitution (if one is in place), so representa-

22

tional images derive from abstract ones. I know, of course, that abstraction appeared long after figuration. As it happens, much American law went on the books before our constitution took effect. However, I'm thinking here about logical relations. Whenever a constitution was ratified, it forms a basis. The legal code is the superstructure, therefore logically subsequent. Though it may have roots in medieval traditions of English common law, an American statute derives its legitimacy from a document only two centuries old.

Similarly, the work of a contemporary figure painter may have evolved from Renaissance tradition, yet it must now draw its esthetic credibility from links to the abstract art that appeared about seven decades ago. That is because, like a constitution well-reasoned from a tradition of law, abstraction gathered from representation all it needed to provide a formal basis for images of the figure in space. The architecture of Scully's imagery suggests that he intuited the relation of abstract to figure painting, and chose to paint abstractly because he wants to work on the foundation of painting, not its superstructure. He wants to be a painter who proposes amendments to painting's constitution.

An ambition that grand reaches past the immediacies of painting to general questions about order in the facades and interiors, the cities and land-scapes—and the pictures—of Western civilization. Our notions of formal har-mony shape what we understand of Newton's universe. Reciprocally, Newtonian images of action, reaction, and equilibrium guide us in making sense of the pictorial order we inherit from antiquity, by way of the Renaissance. Thus a museum docent's account of a neoclassical composition might employ images of force and counterforce, dynamism and balance, that would be equally useful in describing the solar system. A slight shift in terms gives us the checks and balances crucial to the design of modern constitutions.

In one of his *Federalist* papers, Alexander Hamilton argued that "legisla-tive balances and checks" function best in large nations. To those who feared that the American constitution would oppress small, local constituencies, he replied that the opposite is true: essential to the proper functioning of legislature, judiciary, and executive is "the ENLARGEMENT of the ORBIT within which such systems are to revolve"—a thoroughly Newtonian image. [8] James Madison delighted in the picture of "opposite and rival interests" clashing at the highest levels of government and "in all the subordinate distributions of power," for conflicts like these produce their own resolutions. They produce equilibrium, or so he argued. [9]

Madison's devotion to the principle of checks and balances reveals his Newtonian view of the world and of psyches. It also shows a taste for diversity harmonized by the authority of an overarching system—in short, a taste for traditional composition. He helped promulgate what I call the Framers' Esthetic, which was original only in making so nearly explicit the affinities between

Newtonian equilibrium, the idea of balance in the American constitution, and the formal order of properly composed pictures. Though he was not among the framers of the Constitution, Thomas Jefferson had a firm command of this esthetic. He also had a sly knack for subverting its seeming certainties.

In his sketch of his fellow-Virginians' efforts to devise a state constitution, Jefferson wrote that they wanted to establish a government "which should not only be founded on free principles; but in which the powers of government should be so divided and balanced among the several bodies of magistracy as that no one could transcend their legal limits without being effectually checked and restrained by the others." [10] Nothing here is obviously exceptionable, yet with the phrase "free principles" Jefferson put into play a motif that troubles the harmonies of the Framer's Esthetic. This is the motif of civil rights, which still generates unresolvable conflicts between individuals and institutions. When Madison questioned him about the newly proposed constitution, Jefferson said he liked it well enough. Then he pronounced it unacceptable without a bill of rights to guarantee writs of habeas corpus, freedom of religion and the press, and so on. [11] Others made the same objection, sometimes desperately. Still, the constitution took effect without civil rights explicitly guaranteed.

Two years later, the first ten amendments supplied a Bill of Rights. Now there were, in effect, two American constitutions. The first and most powerful one establishes governmental institutions and regulates their workings. This constitution takes note of individuals, but only indirectly, as citizens represented by legislators and subject to the authority of laws as written by Congress, administered by the executive, and adjudicated by the courts. The Bill of Rights, which I am calling the other constitution, acknowledges individuals directly, for its only purpose is to protect their liberties. Yet it is far less powerful than the main body of the constitution. Chiefly, the Bill of Rights authorizes the means to disrupt the workings of governmental institutions when they feel oppressive.

Say the main constitution is a Newtonian machine. An individual seeking redress for violated rights is a part that doesn't fit, an impediment to the smooth meshing of governmental gears. See the constitution as the masterpiece of the Framer's Esthetic, and individuals demanding their rights look like elements with no harmonious place in the composition. To find a place, the individual must let the machinery of checks and balances produce an adjustment. The small unit must let compromise shape it to the large, overarching structure. But appeals to the Bill of Rights insist that some matters allow no compromise because certain values are absolute. Freedom of speech and religion cannot—or should not—be qualified by the give and take of political expediency. So the differences between the main body of the constitution and its first ten amendments have never been reconciled in principle—nor on the plane of esthetics.

Whatever its size, every detail in the allover field claims an absolute value not subject to compromise. Here you find only space and local incident: no stable scale, no firm boundaries, no principles of subordination. Because it is potentially infinite, the allover field has room for any contingency except formal devices of the kind that generate compositional order. Putting on display a pictorial equivalent to the absolutist politics of individual rights, alloverness reconstituted the image of Western culture.

Henry McBride thought Pollock's drip paintings had bombed compositional structure, leveling it to flatness. Resisting the glamour of apocalypse, Ernst Gombrich argued that the painter's snarls of pigment provide us with a humanizing image to project onto "the intricate and ugly shapes with which industrial civilization surrounds us." [12] At the center, order holds; on the margins, alloverness helps us to cast urban decay into an esthetic light. But the allover field is not marginal. It provides a full-scale alternative to composition, or did, until it became one style-option among many. Scully's paintings reanimate this option's larger meanings by returning it to conflict with composition. Invaded by allover fields, Scully's compositions do not fall into ruin. Instead, they try to enclose the field in a bounded structure, at least provisionally. So his pictures constitute themselves as emblems of the clash between the absolutist individual, at home only in alloverness, and institutional order, which finds its most flattering reflection in a well-balanced composition. Leaving it to each of us to imagine a resolution of this conflict, he is an ironic constitutionalist.

To note what is a fiction and what is not: Scully is of course only metaphorically a framer of constitutions, yet the constitutive power of his art is real, and what it constitutes is not merely a basis for painting. Art like his helps shape the culture that shapes us. To see Scully's paintings thoroughly is to watch one's perceptions of order and contingency undergo amendment. It is to become conscious of becoming more conscious. It is to become more alert.

Each of his pictures displays his constitutionalism in a different mood. *White Window* (Fig. 2) gives it a spooked sort of grandeur. In *Us*, (Fig. 1) it is sober and sunlit. *Why and What Yellow* (Fig. 10) is a hectic picture. With its inset of steel, it frames our culture and us as riven, yet skittishly centripetal. This proliferation of nuance may seem to fit awkwardly with Scully's interest in large matters: aren't constitutions supposed to be general, laws specific? Yes and no. A constitution must have wide application, as an abstract painting must be susceptible to many interpretations if it is not to count merely as a design. Yet constitutional precepts are as specific as laws. The difference lies in the grander scale, the richer implication, of constitutional detail.

*

Unlike Scully, most artists who make large proposals about the shape of Western culture mix their abstractions with pictures of recognizable things. In

25

various mediums, including video, Robert Longo arranges bits of standard compositions in rickety structures. Fragments of movies and advertisements; make-believe logos of the blank, corporate kind; images of landscape, usually devastated; dense, monochrome fields of texture; human figures in various states of extremity, violent or numb—these elements of Longo's art argue with their variety that our moment, the source of this plenitude, must be vast. It must lack any principle of decorous order. Therefore it must be an allover field. Longo constitutes selfhood as a survival mechanism rendered heroic by default—that is, by the absence of any credible structure larger than the self. The difficulty is in knowing whether he scatters the self in bits among the season's image-fragments or focuses it in the invisible will that navigates the field.

Sigmar Polke looked as hard at the art of Jackson Pollock as Longo or Scully did. To American eyes, his laminated images look at first like allover fields crowded with detritus from media factories on both sides of the Atlantic. Then one sees the irony in Polke's alloverness. His layered motifs snag one another, drawing the eye to points that anchor compositions of a complexity that earns the right to be called rococo. Pushed toward hysteria by despair, Polke holds out for traditional order, but not reproachfully, not as a criticism of what many Europeans see as American disorder. Polke's pictorial structures have a rueful quality, as if he were resigned to the persistence of composition in his art. He understands the allover field, obviously, but understands just as clearly that American freedoms would look like affectations if they appeared in his art. So he limits himself to freedoms of style and attitude and meaning compatible with Old World order.

From Pollock's drip paintings, Anselm Kiefer extracted an image not of Hiroshima but of Germany destroyed. His allover fields suggest his country reduced to a mud field. As a figure-painter, he devised an iconography calculated to cast German history in a favorable light—or a light as favorable as even a zealous patriot could reasonably demand. As an abstractionist, he proposes an authoritarian constitution, not when he scatters straw across an allover field, but when he clamps the field in a network of orthogonals, the perspective lines that Renaissance painters invented to provide an armature for compositional varia-tion. Kiefer's receding orthogonals impose a rigid governance. Or, to put it the other way around, his compositions oppress the play of contingency that Polke, Longo, and Scully encourage in their differing ways.

Belligerently indifferent to Europe and its ideals of order, Pollock's drip paintings constitute America as a zone of unbounded possibility, utopian or terrifying, according to one's temperament. Setting temperament aside (choos-ing, that is, not to be merely a self-expressive artist), Scully positioned himself to see that, despite its constitutive power, alloverness does not offer an entirely

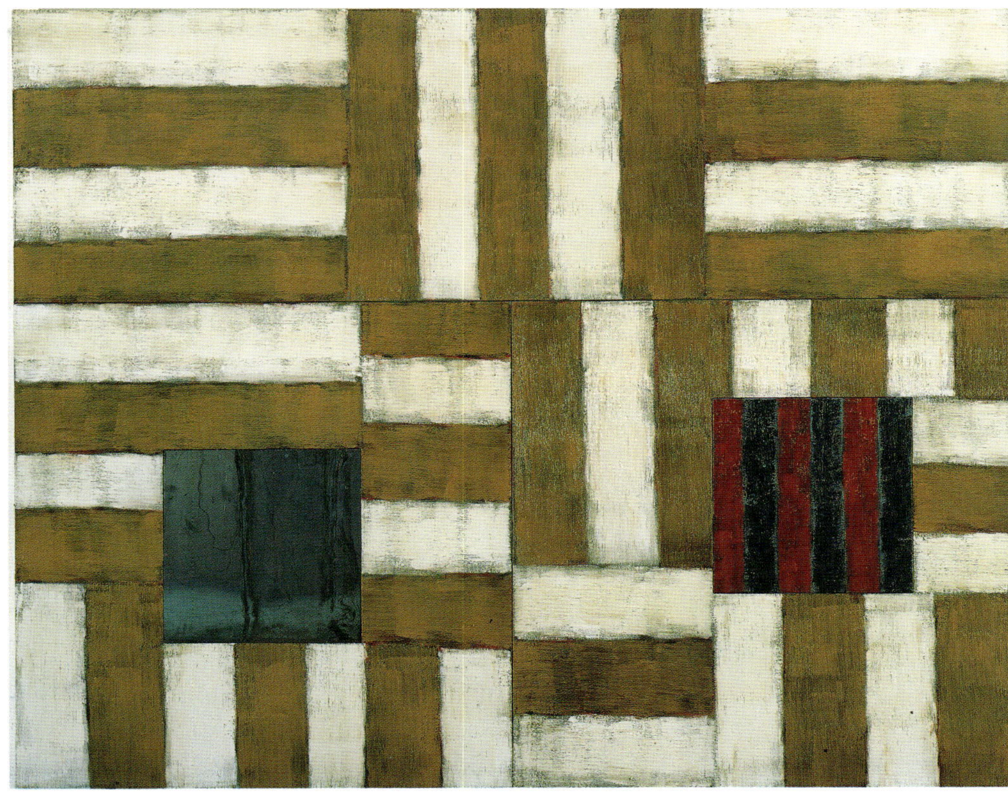

Figure 10. Sean Scully, *Why and What (Yellow)*, 1988
Oil on canvas, 96 x 120 inches.

persuasive definition of the New World. In America, too, Western notions of
harmony and limitation persist. After all, ideals of pictorial order are as intelli-
gible here as in their Mediterranean places of origin.

Estranged even from Pollock's estrangement, Scully argues with his
striped and paneled paintings that alloverness did not supplant composition. His
pictures argue also that the two ways of making a picture cannot be reconciled.
Nor can either be discarded, for each has a legitimate claim to constitute the
form of Western space, history, and culture. In negotiating this irreconcilability,
Scully produces the grand and exemplary conflicts of his paintings. Reflecting
the fragmented state of our institutions and our selves, his art proposes that we
find unity in a full acknowledgment of our condition. His paintings constitute
America as the place where extremes of disunity offer the chance for extremes of
consciousness, and they constitute consciousness as redemption.

I don't say that Scully could have understood art as constitutive only by
immigrating to the United States, with its written constitution and its persistent
appeals to the notion of constitutionality. Modernist ambition requires the artist
to propose a structure for the world, for perception, and for links between them.
When de Stijl, the Surrealists, the Futurists, and other bands of European avant-
gardists issued manifestos, they proposed constitutions for the republic of art.
Yet I think Scully knew that his constitutive impulses would find encouragement

in America, where constitutionality is attacked as often as it is proclaimed, and definitions of every sort are incessantly contended. Alloverness appeared here, arguing from the first that nothing is not provisional, especially individuality. So this is where he settled, to see how Western culture at its most contingent might be constituted, and to join in its constitution.

NOTES

1. Sean Scully, "Berkeley Lecture," unpublished typescript, October 1987, p. 8.

2. This and all subsequent uncited remarks by the artist are from conversations with the author that took place in New York from December 1987 to November 1988.

3. Leon Battista Alberti, *On Painting* (1435-36), trans, John R. Spencer (New Haven: Yale University Press, 1966), pp. 70, 75.

4. David Hume, "Of Simplicity and Refinement in Writing" (1741), *Essays: Moral, Political, and Literary*, ed. Eugene F. Miller (Indianapolis: Liberty Classics, 1985), p. 194.

5. Henry McBride, "Jackson Pollock" (1949) *The Flow of Art: Essays and Criticisms of Henry McBride*, ed. Daniel Catton Rich (New York: Atheneum, 1975) p. 425.

6. Ralph Waldo Emerson, quoted in George M. Frederickson, *The Inner War: Northern Intellectuals and the Crisis of the Union* (New York, 1965), p. 54.

7. Sean Scully and Joseph Masheck, "Piecing Things Together," *Sean Scully: Paintings 1985-1986*, exhibition catalogue (New York: David McKee Gallery, 1986), n. p.

8. Alexander Hamilton, "The Federalist No. 9" (1787), *The Federalist*, ed. Jacob E. Cook (Wesleyan University Press, 1961), p. 52.

9. James Madison, "The Federalist No. 51" (1788), *The Federalist*, p. 349.

10. James Madison, "The Federalist No. 48" (1788), *The Federalist*, p. 335.

11. Thomas Jefferson, letter to James Madison, December 20, 1787, *Thomas Jefferson: Writings* (New York: The Library of America, 1984), pp. 915-16.

12. E. H. Gombrich, *Art and Illusion: A Study in the Psychology of Pictorial Representation* (Princeton, New Jersey: Princeton University Press, 1961), p. 287.

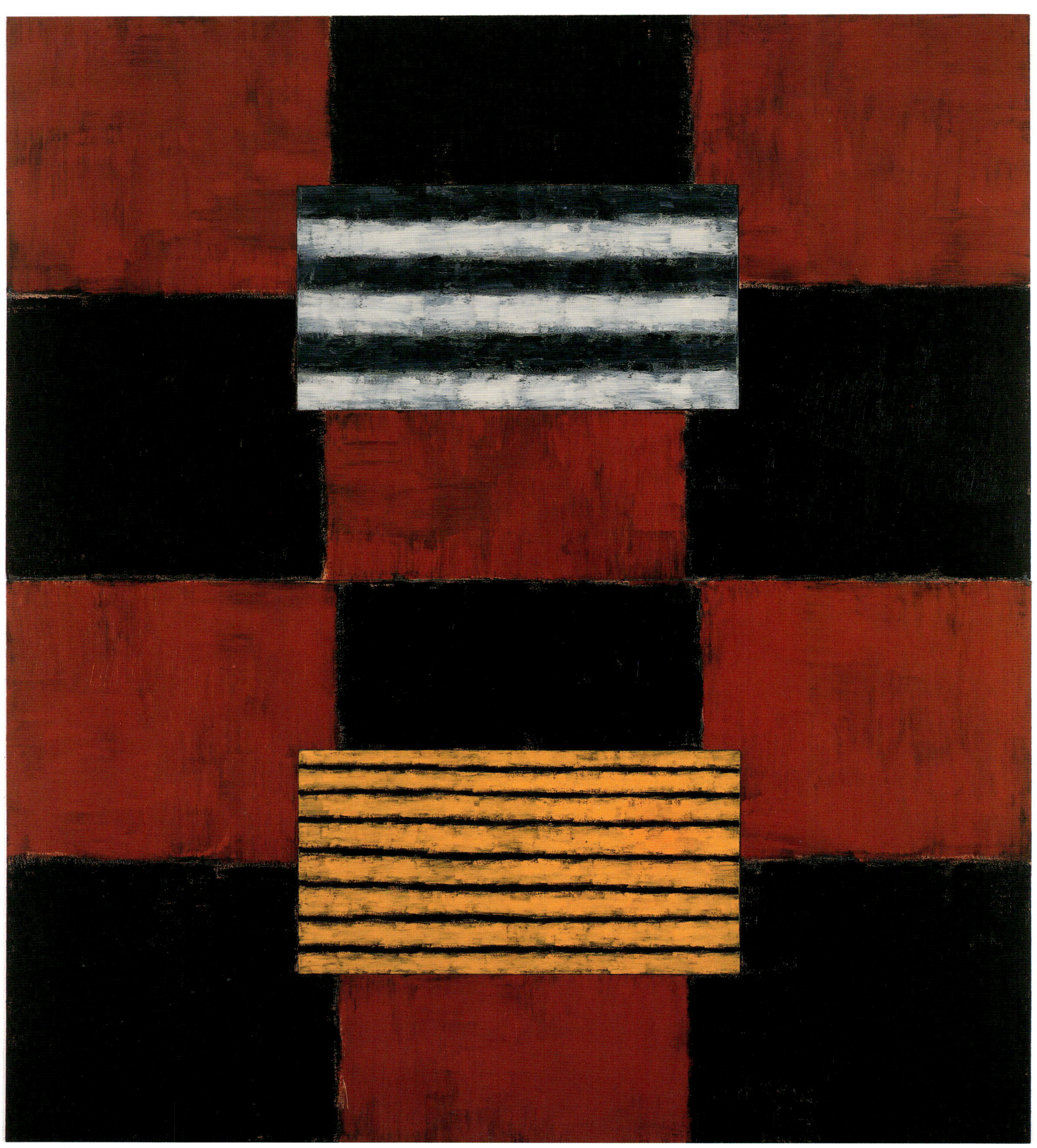

Sean Scully, *Catherine,* 1991
Oil on canvas
100 x 88 inches (254 x 223 cm.)(two panels)

Sean Scully's *Catherine Paintings*:
The Aesthetics of Sequence
by Arthur C. Danto

There was a time when paintings at an exhibition were hung all up and down the walls of a salon, but the common practice today is to install them in single rows around a gallery, placed next to one another with a generous amount of space between. Still, we do not ordinarily begin our visit with the painting next to the entrance, and then work our way in a linear fashion from work to work in the order in which they are displayed. We may find that a certain work attracts us immediately, and we head for it, taking in the rest of the works as we move in irregular diagonals back and forth between the walls. It is a known truth of ophthalmology that in looking at something—a painting only for example—the eye executes what are known as visual *saccades*, leaping from point to point over the surface until the whole is stored, so to speak, in consciousness. But we also move in space saccadically, like a foraging animal, and this is vividly the case in visiting galleries of art. So the order in which works are experienced will vary from person to person, even though each of us stores in memory the exhibition as a whole. We store it in the sense that we remember what we saw but not necessarily the order in which we saw it.

This is because the order in which paintings are hung is merely a convention, and conventions change. And there is no reason for them not to change, since typically there is no internal relationship between the works which are intended to be experienced, aesthetically, one at a time. And in general the order in which these experiences had is not itself part of the experience. One might say, in effect, that a succession of aesthetic experiences, is not an aesthetic experience of succession. When, on the other hand, as with the *Catherine Paintings* of Sean Scully, the works are understood to form a series, then the experience of any one of them must be more complex than that of a single painting, just because the fact that each is part of the series must enter somehow as part of the experience of each. They retain their individual authority—and as we shall see, their doing so is a condition for being part of the series to begin with—and so in experiencing any of them we do not do so with the sense that we are confronting the fragment of some larger whole. But even so the knowledge that there is a larger whole of which they are successive parts must count as part of our understanding, especially when the circumstances of exhibition permits us to see them all together, and as forming an evolving totality. We want at the very least to know what principle generates the series and determines what it means for a painting to be part of it.

Websters defines a series as "A number of things or events of the same class coming one after the other in spatial or temporal succession." So we want to know in virtue of what property the *Catherine Paintings* form a class—we want to know in what "catherinity" consists. And then we want to know what determined the artist to add paintings to this class "one after the other in temporal succession," as the dictionary has it, so that they compose a series. We want further to know what this knowledge is meant to add to our experiences of these works taken one at a time. It is a particularly rare occasion when we can see works spanning fourteen years by an artist whose maturity coincides with these works chronologically in such a way that the works virtually serve as a transcript of this maturation. Still, that might be the case with any retrospective of Scully's work if sufficiently representative. But such a retrospective would lack the intended unity in the sequence when this is not simply the unity of the life of the artist but rather, formally, more like the unfolding of a narrative. Still, the sequenced members of the *Catherine* series do not occur in anything like that in which the successive paintings do in Rubens's depiction of stages in the life of Maria de Medici in the Louvre, for example. So there is a first painting, which begins the series, but it is not a beginning in the classical sense in which stories have beginnings, middles, and ends, as these are discussed in Aristotle's *Poetics*. The series will stop with a certain painting, but that painting will not be an ending as, say, the Apotheosis of Maria de Medici concludes the epic of her life and of Rubens's series.

This singular exhibition of all the *Catherine Paintings* gives an occasion for us to reflect on the different ways in which paintings can occur in ordered

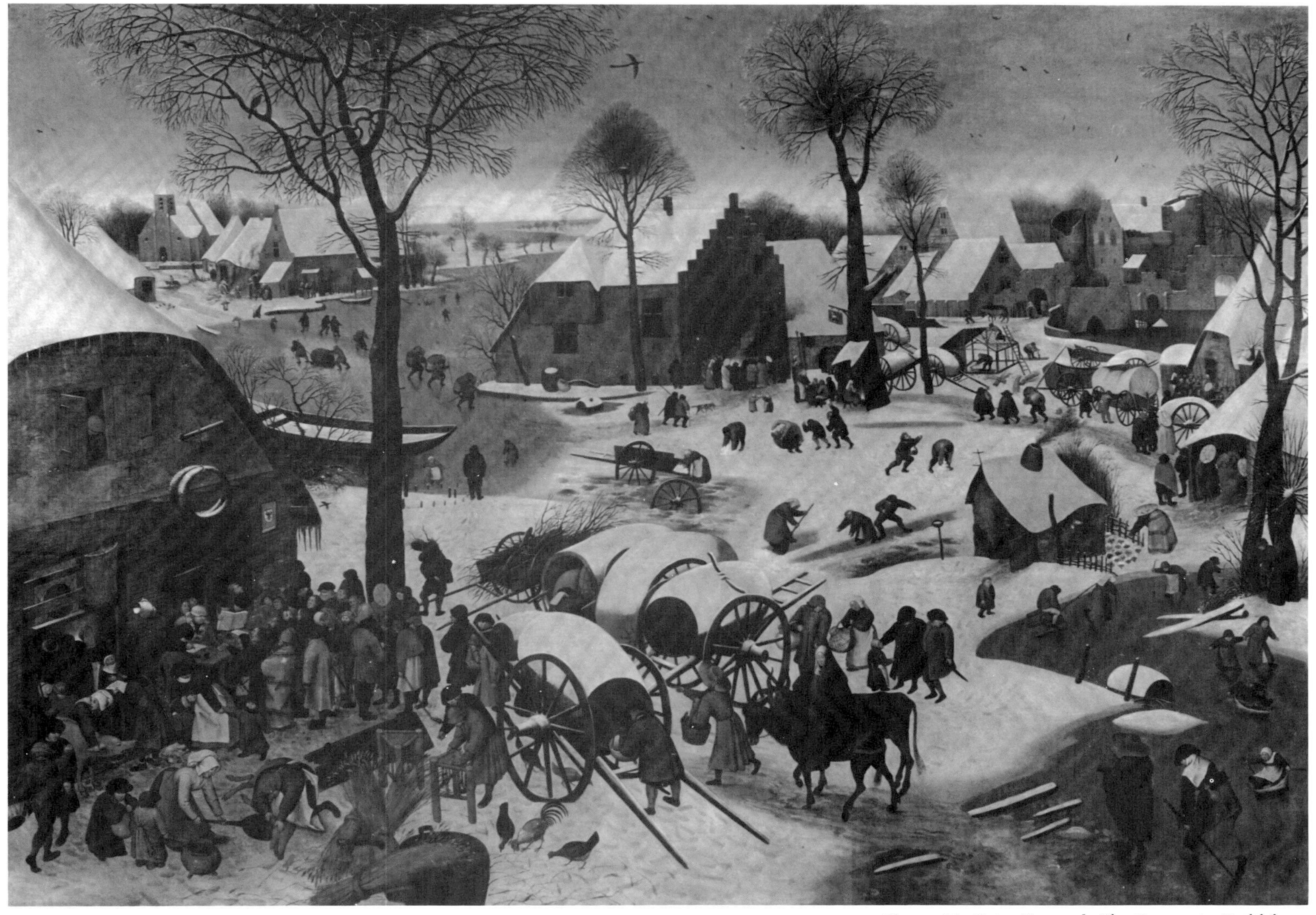

Figure 11. Peter Bruegel, *The Census in Bethlehem*, Bonnefantenmuseum, Maastricht, The Netherlands, Collection R.B.K.

sets. I shall return to the *Catherines* when I have canvassed something of the logic and then the aesthetics of seriality.

*

In the Bonnefantenmuseum in Maastricht, in the Netherlands, there is a characteristic painting by Pieter Bruegel called *The Census in Bethlehem*, (Fig. 11) thronged with episode and incident, crowded with figures bent upon business fateful and not so fateful. It shows, at its compositional or at least moral center, Saint Joseph, shouldering his carpenter's saw and pointing his wife's gaze toward an inn, where the animals she is to bed down with await them. The painting has a Christmas card quality which must have been found as charming by Bruegel's contemporaries as it is by us, for there exist, I was told by the museum's director, no fewer than thirteen known instances of this painting from Bruegel's work-

33

shop. It is almost as if there were something like a pattern book there from which clients could order paintings, and *The Census in Bethlehem* turned out to be a particularly popular item. It clearly no more detracted from the enjoyment purchasers took in the paintings they bought that there were other and perhaps a great many other copies of the work than it especially bothers us that the Christmas cards we buy and send exist in the thousands. But at the same time the knowledge that there were others relevantly just like it could not have been part of the experience of the work. The thirteen known instances of *The Census in Bethlehem* do not form a series.

This does not mean that were all thirteen hung in a stunning exhibition, one could not, were one concerned with connoisseurship, trace minute changes or the presence of different hands. Or one could perhaps identify a development, providing the chronology, presumably based upon archival findings, could be established. But the experience of the connoisseur, or even the art historian concerned with the fixing of chronological sequence, would have very little to do with the terms in which the painting, in any or in all of its exemplification, are to be appreciated. For they have little to do with the incidents in which Joseph, uxorious and steady, steers his pregnant wife toward the manger of her delivery. The set of exemplars stand to one another as the prints do in an edition, except that there is no plate to guarantee sameness of image from exemplar to exemplar, and degradations in which make it imperative for the collector to know which came first or at least earlier in the sequence of impressions.

It follows that a painting is part of a series when the knowledge that it is so is part of the experience of the individual works that form that series (in the Bruegel case, the knowledge that a painting is popular may confirm one's taste but not transform the set of paintings which prove its popularity into a series). Even so, it is important that we distinguish the series from at least two other kinds of ordered sets: from the *sequence,* which I have touched on already in the case of Maria de Medici, and from the *suite,* both of which have played an important role in artistic production. The sequence is defined by a narrative structure, and it is certainly true that the knowledge that a given painting forms part of a sequence penetrates our experience of it because we know it tells only part of the story, and in that sense is incomplete. But that means that in order to be experienced under the category of completeness, we must have some sense of what the other elements in the sequence are, and where this one fits in with them. For example, the oxherd riding the ox is always an affecting image even in isolation from the oxherding sequence which condenses so much of the teaching of Zen. But it lacks the profundity it acquires when seen as part of a sequence in which the oxherd undergoes an abrupt illumination, and in which we see him at the end as a sage old man in the wilderness. The response to the oxherding pictures is reenactment, they themselves are guides to the sort of enlightenment

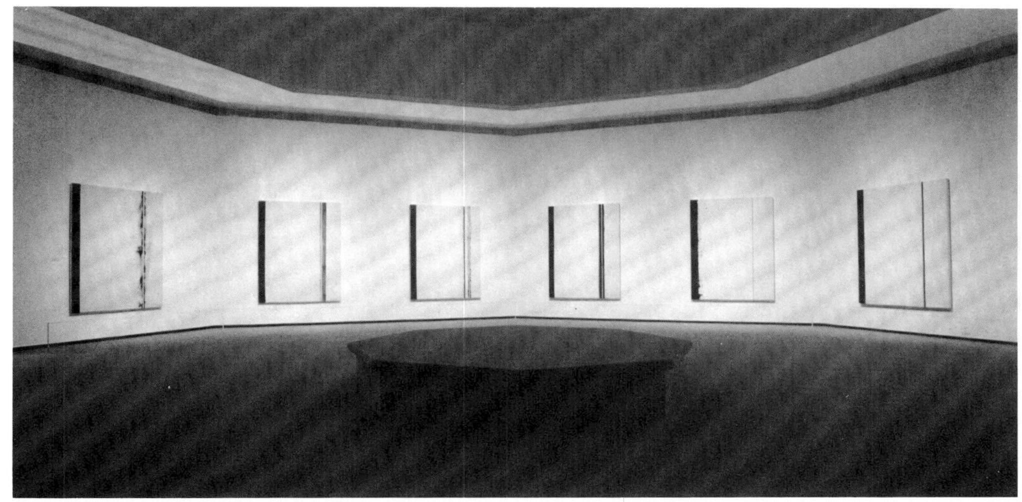

Figure 12. Installtion view, Barnett Newman, *Stations of the Cross*, 1958-62 (*First* through *Sixth Station*), National Gallery of Art, Washington, Robert and Jane Meyerhoff Collection.

they also show, and the viewer is to use them as a kind of spiritual prosthetic, with which to proceed from stage to stage of spiritual ascent. The same of course is true of the Fourteen Stations of the Cross. Any one of the images in the series is the subject of innumerable representations in the west, where Crucifixions or Descents or Entombments have been commissioned or purchased for specific sites and purposes. But when a Crucifixion is part of the sequence, one is to have arrived at it by having first passed through the preceding stations, in which it constitutes a climax: the various falls, the kindly intervention of Saint Veronica, the *mise au Tombeau*. And there is accordingly an experience had in viewing it which will differ from viewing some artist's Descent from the Cross in isolation, even if one's meditation on this event is the same as one might have undergone in a sequence of meditations which map on to the Stations. No one who has seen Barnett Newman's *Stations of the Cross* (Fig. 12) would have felt that it little mattered, since the paintings are abstract, that they should be shown as an ensemble or dissolved into component works and distributed between various museums. There is, for example, a point at which the white-on-black is reversed to black-on-white, and the reversal is so powerful that one is obliged to read it as the moment of transfigurative agony attained to by Christ: it is virtually as if one saw it as the outward embodiment in painterly terms of an internal spiritual crisis.

The Stations of the Cross exists in as many as fifteen paintings (when one adjoins the discovery of the cross Saint Helena), or in as few as eleven paintings, as in the order of the Diocese of Vienna. But the narrative defines what it means for a sequence to be ordered and for something to belong to it or not: "Something which . . . explains nothing else is no part of the whole," Aristotle writes. It also specifies beginnings and endings. Hogarth's *The Rake's Progress* describes an itinerary of degradation, and *Marriage a la Mode* an itinerary of dissolution: we know that the one has to end with a death of a particularly cautionary sort, and the other with divorce and infidelity. What I shall call a *suite* may be narratively driven, but in general the images in a suite will illustrate a text or theme, and will not themselves compose a narrative even if the text itself is a narrative. This, for example, would be the case with Botticelli's illustrations to the Divine Comedy, where one has to know where a certain picture fits the text in order to understand it, but where there can be no adequate experience of the various images without external reference to the text which unites them. Botticelli's drawings would often be genuinely puzzling had the famous poem disappeared, or if one did not know there was a poem which explains them. And by comparison with the life of Christ, the story is not so widely known that it can be taken for granted, and in any case the pictures are too visually eccentric to imagine them standing alone, as with the Crucifixion of the Descent. The same is true of the body of etchings furnished by Georges Rouault for Les reencarnations du Pere Ubu, where the text by Alfred Jarry is exceedingly rarified and known to a far smaller number than those who may know Rouault's images. There is, so far as I know, no narrative whatever which drives the so-called Vollard Suite (Fig. 13) of etching done by Picasso between 1930 and 1947, though there is a unifying theme, having to do with the sculptor and the sculptor's studio. There is moreover a great deal of variation in style and in explicit subject matter from one end to the other of the suite, but no necessary order of a kind that would enable us to think of them as forming a sequence. So I define a suite as several works illustrating if not a text then a theme, and with no particular similarity from image to image other than those which pertain to the artist's style. Thus Goya's *Los Disastros de la Guerra* is a suite, as is his *Los Capriccios.* It is perhaps because we think of their number and variety that we count Botticelli's *Divine Comedy* illustrations as composing a suite rather than a sequence, despite the narrative structure of the poem itself.

Suites and sequences form wholes and have a certain unity which applies to wholes. This is not obviously true of *series,* which can be open, and can be held to be complete at any point, or, by the same criterion, as always incomplete. The unity of the sequence is the unity of the action the viewer is able to recover in experiencing the members of the sequence in, well, sequential order. The unity of the suite can be referred to the unity of the text the individual components of the suite subserve, or to a certain thematic unity, or to a stylistic unity, within which there may be room for considerable variety. A suite of furniture, if we may take that as a model for the concept, is unified by the inter-related functions of the elements of the suite, defined often or typically be a form of life: the bed, the chaise lounge, the armoire, the dressing table define the life of the bedroom; the sofa, the arm chairs, the deal table, the vitrine the life of the parlor. But it would ordinarily not be counted a suite if there were not some further unity, such as that of style or material. Mel Bochner's *Wittgenstein Drawings* compose a suite,

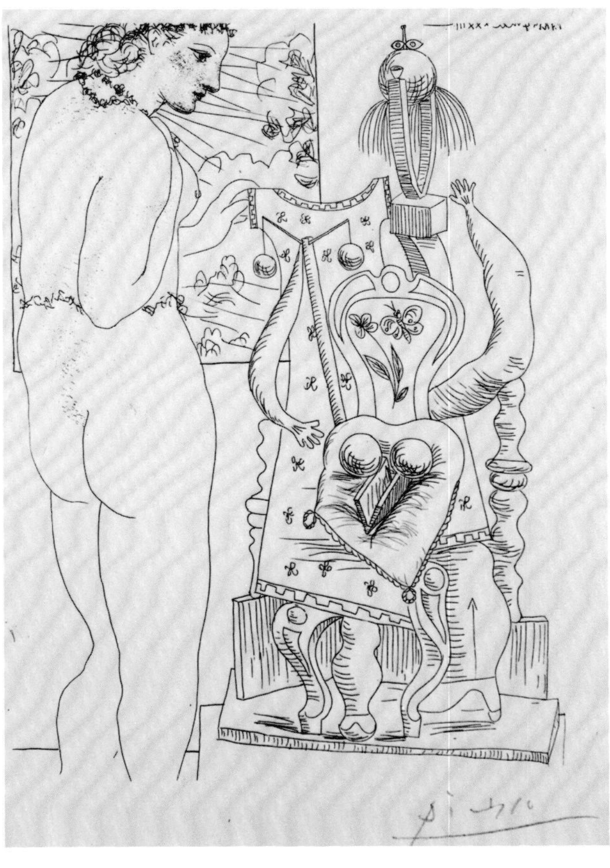

Figure 13. Pablo Picasso, *May 4, 1933*, from the Vollard Suite
Etching, 10 ½ inches x 7 5/8 inches
Collection of the Modern Art Museum of Fort Worth,
Museum Purchase, The Benjamin J. Tillar Memorial Trust.

rather than a sequence, because there is a text by Wittgenstein which they
illustrate, and where the works in part are generated by the problem of how one
illustrates a philosophical text. There is a unity in the drawings, in that they use,
invariantly, the same form as a frame—a square whose corners and the mid-
points of whose edges are connected—and numerals. The variety comes in with
the order in which the numerals are written, which will differ from drawing to
drawing.

Both sequences and suites may be found quite far back in the history of
art, East as well as West. The stations of the Cross is a Franciscan ceremony,
while a set of portraits of Christ and the disciples constitutes a suite in a well-
known Byzantine embroidery. *The Progress of Love* by Fragonard is a sequence,
the panels done by Boucher for the boudoir of Madame Pompadour of the four
seasons is a suite, limited and defined by the number of the seasons and what the
defining activities are of each of them. But the idea of a *series* seems to me to
refer us to the artist in a special way, and I am not certain how deep into history
one can go to find precedents for the great series of modern art. In the 1890s, of
course, Monet did a great many series, and it really was important for viewers to
understand that the individual paintings in them belonged to a series, even if it
would be rare, after the first exhibition of them, to see the series in its entirety.

Each of the series had to do with the fall of light on surfaces, and so could be counted observations made sequentially of how light modified form, and hence to the artist who made and recorded the observations, whether of the facade of Rouen cathedral, or of grainstacks at Giverny, or the banks of the Creuse, or whatever. And indeed it was in part to appropriate to his work the connotations of science and of cognitive process that Monet undertook the exceedingly strenuous tasks achieving the series exacted: carrying multiple canvases, lifting them on and off the easel as the sun moved, etc. But Monet's series have affinities with the sequence—since the light changes in the course of the day from early to late—and with the suite—since each series seems to be driven by some concept of a whole, and hence with the ideal of completeness, which does not, as I see it, quite go with the concept of the series. At least it does not go with the two main examples of series in twentieth-century art—Robert Motherwell's *Elegies for the Spanish Republic* and Richard Diebenkorn's *Ocean Park* paintings. Nor does it go, as we shall see, with Sean Scully's *Catherine Paintings,* which we may place alongside them.

It is characteristic of the fact that these are series—rather that sequences or suites—that none of the artists, so far as I know, set out, in doing the first one, with the knowledge that it was the first one, and hence that it was to belong to a series. The thought of the series dawned later. Certainly that was the case with Motherwell. The first *Elegy*—known as *Ink Sketch, Elegy No. 1,* was intended as an illustration for a poem by Harold Rosenberg, which was to have been published in the second issue of a magazine—*Possibilities*—which in fact had only one issue. (It is ironic that magazines, as serial publications, intend that there be a series, as *Possibilities* certainly did—the first and as it happens only issue of the magazine was explicitly identified as *Possibilities I*—but that it was a drawing, intended for publication later in the series, which grew into a series while the magazine did not). Motherwell, according to the monograph devoted to him by Jack Flam, went back to the image a year later, and decided to work it up in casein. And this time it was to illustrate a different poem, *At Five in the Afternoon,* by Federico Garcia Lorca. Motherwell said that it had as its theme "the Spanish idea of death which he got from Lorca, but also from his own experiences in Mexico. But the formal theme obsessed him, and by the time of his death, he had completed over 170 *Elegies,* which more and more came to embody for him a kind of political lamentation, as if for the death of certain political ideals. Any given *Elegy,* from *Ink Sketch No. I* of 1949 to *Elegy for the Spanish Republic (with Blood), No. 172,* of 1990 (Fig. 14), is recognizable as belonging to the same impulse: there are variations in scale and in the number of elements and of colors, but the basic forms remain, of ovals and bars, and the basic black-and-white palette is always present, even if touched in with ochre (sand) or red (blood). Motherwell once told me that he still had not as yet gotten the *Elegy*

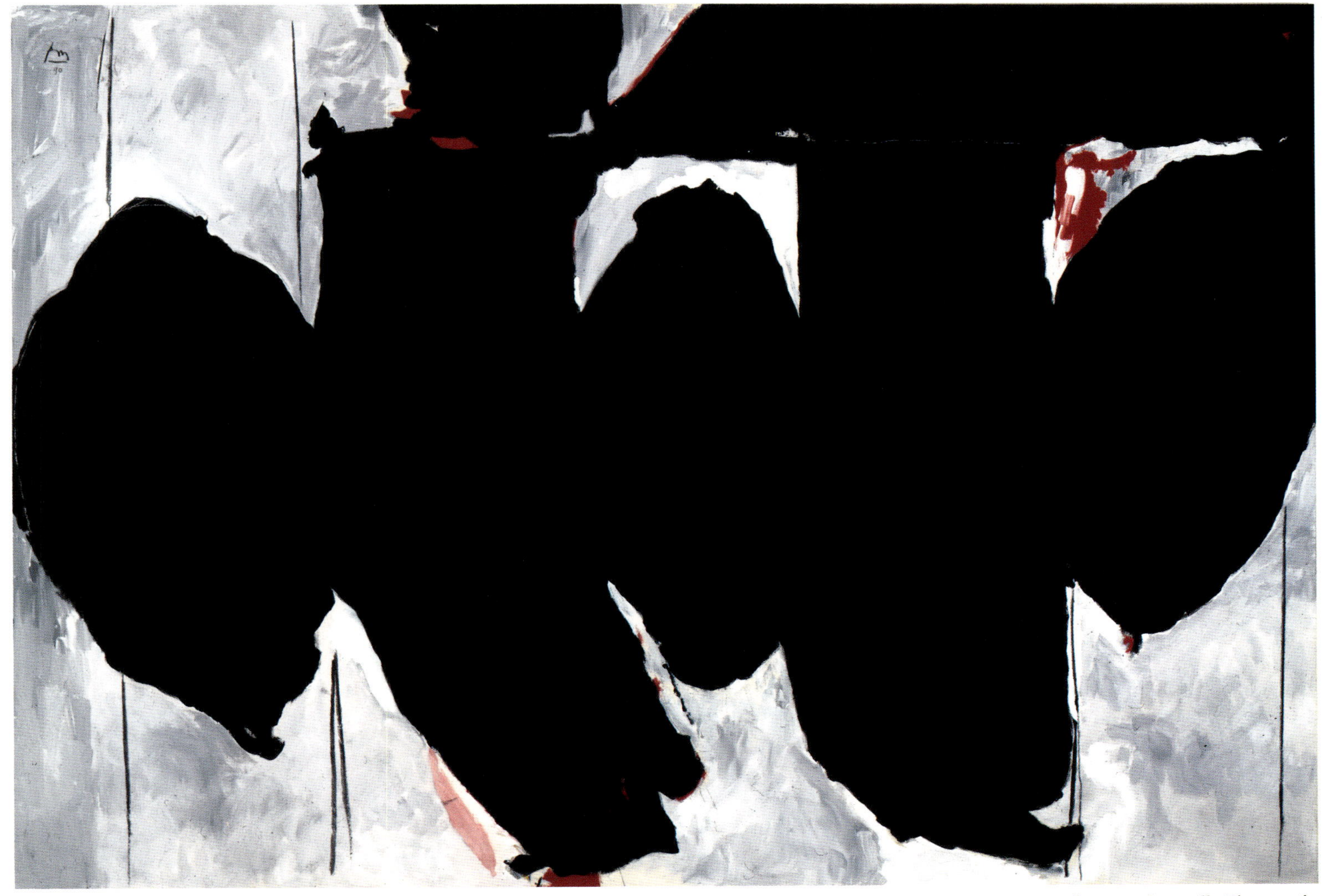

Figure 14. Robert Motherwell, *Elegy to the
Spanish Republic No. 172*, 1989
Acrylic on canvas, 84 x 120 inches,
©1993, Dedalus Foundation

down right, and that it would have ended had he achieved that (my sense is that it would never have ended, because he would have wondered if he could do it again). It was almost as if there were a platonic form of the *Spanish Elegies*, which defines the series from without (or toward which the series converges, if we think of it as mathematical), but there is no real limit on the number of exemplars such a form can generate, and that is one mark of a series: it is numerically open.

It is important to stress that though an abstract painter, Motherwell's impulses came from outside the world of painting—not just from poetry, from publication, and from politics, but from the circumstances of his life: being in Mexico, having a Mexican wife, seeing bullfights, and the rest. Diebenkorn, whose life has been far less epic, is also far more restricted in what he responded to in his art. The *Ocean Park* (Fig. 16) series marks his break with figuration in 1967, and the influence of Matisse is manifest. The title of the individual works—*Ocean Park* with a number—rather than *Untitled—is* perhaps a gesture by some-

39

one who wants to keep some connection with figuration, but whatever poetry the works convey, it cannot be from the kind of poetry that Motherwell's works come. It comes from the pleasure in working with colors, flat forms, and the aims seem largely aesthetic. Diebenkorn was still painting *Ocean Park* works in 1980 (when the series had reached 125) though it would be hard to tell the difference between many of them and paintings he did which were not *Ocean Park* paintings. In any case, I am disinclined to think that Diebenkorn would say he would stop when he got it right. Rather, it is as though Ocean Park specifies some kind of matrix within which the artist is able to paint. It is to the abstract artist what a motif would be to a realist. It would be like Monet's grainstack, a way of painting what he wants to paint. And in fact the *Ocean Park* paintings resemble another series that Motherwell once did more than they do the *Elegies,* and which I once saw in its entirety in his studio. These were the *Night Music* (Fig. 17) collages. He had meant to do only one. But his wife, Renata Ponsold, asked if she could have it, something she had never done before. Motherwell of course gave it to her, but wanted to make one for himself, and he then ran the idea until there were twenty-odd *Night Musics,* and he stopped.

This little anecdote reveals a certain sentimentality in Robert Motherwell's personality (one might have inferred it from the fact that he did a series of paintings in which the chief motif was the French phrase *Je t'aime),* and that gives us an obvious connection to the *Catherine Paintings,* where the title refers to a specific woman, Catherine Lee, who has been Scully's wife since 1978, though the couple lived together for some years before that. And just as I should suppose the *Je t'aime* works do not simply depict the phrase with which love is declared, but in fact are painterly declarations in their own right which use the phrase to do so, the *Catherine* paintings too are acts of celebration of Catherine, and of the relationship in which the artist stands to her, and of the feeling toward her that the designation of the paintings express, whatever the paintings themselves might be said to express. The dedication to a book expresses a complex of feelings the author has toward the dedicatee, whatever the book itself expresses, and something close to this is meant by the fact that the *Catherine Paintings* are addressed to Catherine Lee. They do not refer to her, certainly not in the way in which the *Spanish Elegies* refer to Spain or to the spirit of Spain, nor even in the attenuated way the *Ocean Park*—a residential development north of Los Angeles on the Pacific, where Diebenkorn's studio was located for many years. Indeed, the status of being a *Catherine Painting is conferred* on the paintings which enjoy it, like a title of nobility, whatever the artist may have intended when he first did the painting. At a certain moment the painting is recognized as possessing the qualities Catherine herself possesses in the estimation of the artist, her husband: The *Catherine painting is* to the paintings of a given year by Sean Scully what Catherine is among women: There is an equivalence between the paintings and the woman, which is consistent with the paintings having no overarching formal resemblance, such as the *Elegies* or, for that matter, the *Ocean Park* paintings have. And it is equally consistent with the logic of the series that the *Catherine* Painting of a given year resemble other Scully paintings of that year more than the *Catherine* paintings of other years. In a way, the whole series of *Catherine Paintings* show the development from year to year of the artist's vision. The point is that sometime after the year's paintings are done, Scully and Catherine decide which of them should be the *Catherine* painting for that year. But the criteria on which this is decided makes each painting an uncommon tribute by Scully to the woman who is herself remarkable in his eyes. Just as Scully's work goes far beyond formal explanation though abstract, the *Catherine* paintings express feelings that go well beyond aesthetics.

The first of the paintings in the series was not conceived of as inaugurating a series, nor as a *Catherine* painting. It is work which would rather have to be understood in terms of Scully's artistic projects of the year in which it was done, and it consists in a uniform array of thinnish horizontal stripes, each three-quarters of an inch wide, laid down in a fairly mechanical way, brown-black against blue-grey. There are reasons for everything the painting involves—color, stripes, orientation, shape (which is square), scale, surface quality, touch, sharpness. He had not as yet evolved the signature style of his mature work, with wide bands and vibrant edges and beautiful painting strokes and inserts in which the stripes will sometimes go at right angles to those of the containing work, and have a different color and carry a different meaning. Rather, Scully was involved in work of a certain spare elegance, so conceived and executed as, in his works, to "take the hand out" whereas in the later work everything is done to keep the hand *in*. Scully is cited by Carter Ratcliff as having said that he felt the need, in the 1970s, to "paint severe, invulnerable canvases, so that I could be in this [i.e.

Figure 15. Robert Motherwell, *Study for Elegy to the Spanish Republic No. 100*, 1975, Acrylic on canvas board, 8 ½ x 24 inches, ©1993, Dedalus Foundation

in the New York] environment and not feel exposed. I spent five years making my paintings fortress-like. And indeed one might see the first of the *Catherine* paintings, done in 1979, as at the very end of this defensive agenda: the stripes serve as bars, to keep the hostile environment at bay, to screen intrusion. But all these characterizations serve to explain the work of the entire period. It does not explain why this particular work should have been called *Catherine*. Scully says that at a certain moment he said to himself that this work was "good enough to be a Catherine painting." It was chosen for its aesthetic eminence from among its peers, and whatever motivated it as a painting, what motivated it as having been chosen a Catherine painting was its goodness as art. It was in effect *primus inter pares*. Needless to say, the association between shelter, protection, the admission of vulnerability goes beautifully with what Catherine herself has to have stood for in the psychic economy of Scully's life at that moment: *she* was his fortress and his shield, his armor, his peace.

Scully once said that whereas Motherwell and Diebenkorn are pre-Minimalist painters, he is post-Minimalist, and I suppose this means that the experience of Minimalism exposes his work, especially from the late Seventies, to a severely formal and reduced interpretation whereas in fact its minimalism enable him to exploit a special range of quite human meanings a less austere vocabulary might be unable to express. It is not merely a fact about the paintings that there is no evidence of hand and touch, but part of the content of these works that they make no concession to the tentative, the diffident, the soft, the vague, but have a kind of formal bravado, a kind of front the artist puts up. And stripes themselves are after all not merely stripes: they too have their meanings and their associations, which they bring into the painting form the world without. The porticulus at the entry way through a protective wall too is a grid, dropped into place to keep predators out, to close temporarily the open space through which life flows in and out of the fortified city. "My wife, my shield," is an affecting sentiment, but, being wife and shield, there is beyond that a special beauty to this declaration which is possessed by its peers in some lesser degree. So it rather than they became the *Catherine* painting for 1979, like a prize conferred by the artist on the pick of that year's labor and creation.

The idea of there being a series began to take form when Scully recognized that there must be in any given year one particularly outstanding work, which distilled whatever was at work in his artistic persona in that period, and that expressed it most effectively. The second *Catherine* painting does not carry forward the artist's agenda of the previous period: it is a system of vertical stripes adjoining a system of horizontal stripes, and, standing side by side within the narrow confines of a format two and a third times higher than it is wide, where the space is evenly divided between the vertical being and the horizontal being, the two systems form a couple, each member possessing what the other can

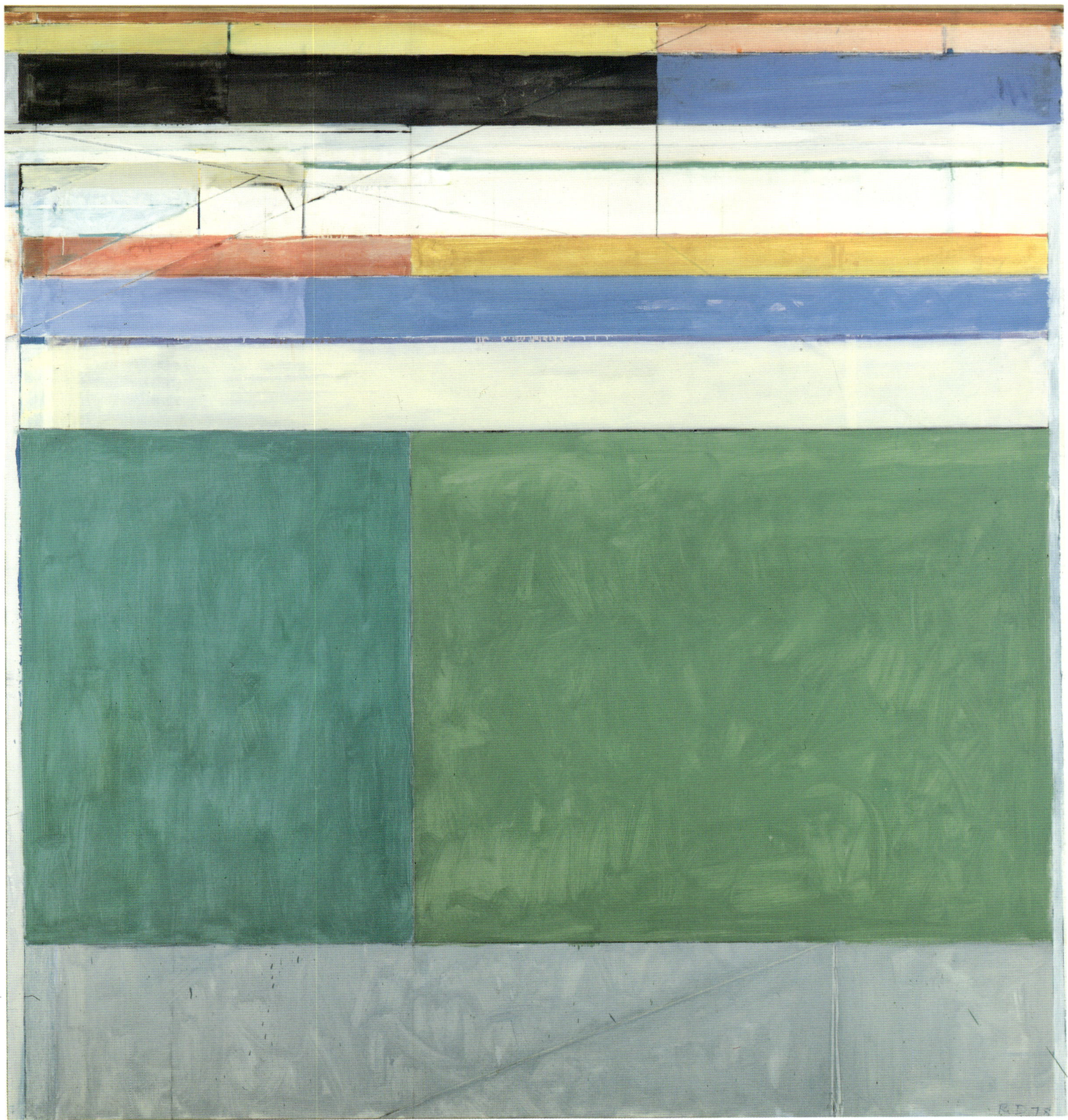

Figure 16. Richard Diebenkorn, *Ocean Park #105*, 1978
Oil and charcoal on canvas, 100 x 93 inches
Museum Purchase, Sid W. Richardson Foundation Endowment Fund
and The Anne Burnett and Charles Tandy Foundation Endowment Fund.

never have, and yet together forming a harmony and a unity. Whatever its connotations, it is no longer a fortress. And in the following year, in 1981, it was as if the walls had come down altogether. The light flowed in and the paintings take on that palpitating quality almost as if their components stripes breath freely, and let their edges soften into one another's territories. Scully has made some kind of internal adjustment, the hand is back, the stripes widen, the colors brighten, and there is an inevitable association with good things, circus tents and beach umbrellas, tigers at the zoo, their stripes dancing past the bars of the cages they pace in—or bars of light falling on the floor as the light streams through the window. By 1981, the project of choosing a *Catherine* painting for each year had become settled.

The first of the *Catherine Paintings* was sold to a close friend—so close, Scully says, that the three of them very nearly were a household. It was returned to Sean and Catherine before the friend's death, by which time the decision had been made not merely to designate a *Catherine Painting* for any given year, but to keep it for the couple's own private collection. I am moved by the thought of keeping, for the marriage itself, the finest work in each year, and see it as an act of renewal and of sacrifice. It is a sacrifice in the way in which the old Greek warriors would sacrifice the fattest meat and the strongest wine to the gods in

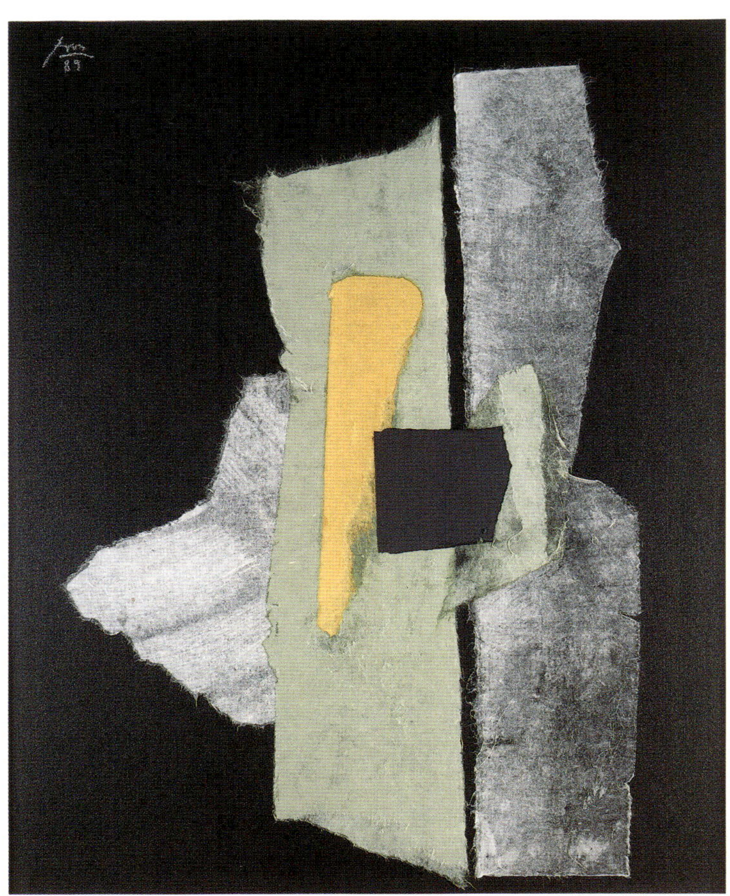

Figure 17. Robert Motherwell, *Night Music, Opus* No. 27, 1988
Acrylic on canvas panel, 32 ¼ x 26 ½ inches,
©1993, Dedalus Foundation

44

order to secure their favor for whatever undertaking was at hand. Here one has withdrawn a painting, like a fatted calf, and dedicated it to the marriage, and not putting it on the market. So the finest work is not for sale, nor will it in fact be sold, for the intention is to offer the entire series to a museum at some point, if the institution agrees to keep the series altogether and in perpetuity. This would not have been possible had so sweeping a decision not been made: no museum could afford to own one of Monet's series, nor the whole of the *Ocean Park* or *Spanish Elegy* series, which have been dispersed among different collections. But perhaps there is not the same reason for even thinking about keeping the latter series together, for while there is variation in scale and in success among the members of the series, one has a very vivid sense of the whole series from one or two exemplars. But this cannot possibly be true of the *Catherine Paintings,* which have no particular formal similarities beyond what defines Scully's work as an evolving whole. Each painting is drawn off, like a wine, and embodies that particular vintage; and though there are, as with wines, those constant factors which make for consistency and greatness, there is also that variety from year to year, that means that one who knows the wine only generically has not taken the measure of its possibilities.

The Spanish Republic is a fixed historical moment, and Ocean Park is a determinant locus in which one expects no great changes in the distribution of sea, shore, and sky. But Catherine Lee is a living person and a growing artist, just as Sean Scully himself is. And the marriage, like any enduring marriage, has its constant adjustments and transformations. So the *Catherine Paintings* incorporate three transformative beings and their relationships. Each painting in the series is, as I have said, a distillation of where and what Scully was as an artist in that year, but the series taken as a whole shows us a great deal more than that. Sometimes, for example, a *Catherine Painting* will belong to a series on which Scully was working in a given year, which only intersects the *Catherine* series, and in consequence has two identities. The 1991 *Catherine,* for example, belongs to a series of paintings about women. There are four of them. Mariana is based on the Infanta as depicted by Velasquez. Lucia is a response to the *Burial of Saint Lucy* by Caravaggio, which belongs to an old church just outside Siracusa, in Sicily, where Scully had painted one summer. And a third work, in black and white stripes, is named after Eve. The 1991 *Catherine* situates the actual person, Catherine Lee, in a particularly exalted female company: a princess; a saint (and one especially relevant to an artist, for her name means light and Lucia's attributes are her eyes); and the Mother of Us All. And there is almost something heraldic in the bold pattern of the checkerboard—which at the very least carries the iconographic meaning that it is a field in which one may be crowned, just as the painting which is catherinized, to coin a term, is in effect coronated. And there are the striped inserts like Palio banners or knightly pennants, which are emblems of celebration and glory. When what turned out to be the *Catherine Painting* was begun, Scully thought it might be the Catherine painting for that year. But of course this is never something to be decided in advance, given the way such decisions are made.

Scully has been a resolute abstractionist for the better part of his career, but he is in no sense a formalist, and there are all sorts of clues to how a painting is to be understood in terms of the atmosphere of meanings its forms carry and imply. Scully is extremely forthcoming on these matters, for he is anxious to be understood and in particular not to be misunderstood. His concern is to communicate as much as anything else. But he is also an extremely personal artist, and this dimension of his art comes forward in an especially vivid way with the *Catherine Paintings. As* a series, it has the kind of meaning a life has, in the sense that in living into the future, we redefine our pasts. Scully cannot know the shape of his own future any more than any of us can know the shape of ours, but that means that he cannot foresee the forward shape of the *Catherine* series for what will enter into the next member belongs to the creative resources of time to come. Life is defined by uncertainty and risk, but also by a kind of unity which settles over it and gives it a certain shape. Scully has allowed the logical features of lived life to operate over the series of his best efforts, and this gives it a quality unique in the annals of modern art. One cannot but wish for the artist—and for ourselves—that the series go on and on!

Wholeness, Partness, and the Gift
by Steven Henry Madoff

A man and a woman fall in love. The world falls away. Her face is
extraordinary. He thinks it absorbs every inflection of his thought. He is no less
fascinating to her—a giver of sympathy, amusement. Then they come to know
each other. It turns out that she has her habits, her small gestures that annoy
him, but he has to grow used to them because, after all, she is the loved one.
He's just as vagrant. There are often times she needs something that he can't
give, that he's unwilling to give. Of course, it's the same with her. The endless
details of this relationship, this life together as it builds, falls apart, goes on—it's
full of warmth and bitterness, embrace and retreat, lightness and dark.

For the pleasure of invention, of fantasy—since that's one of the great
satisfactions of art—I imagine this story, I begin a tale. I find it here, in this first
picture by Sean Scully, this dark one that utters the opening words. It's as if the
first "Catherine" painting has been brought into existence from the chaos of all
that has come before for the artist: his earlier pictures; his appreciation, specifically here, of Frank Stella's "Black Paintings" of the early 1960s; the lovers in his
past. Out of these memories—these emotions, disturbances, knowledge—his

"Catherine" painting emerges, barely more than the darkness of that tumult of the past, that universe information.

Yet the darkness has been arranged, brought into order. The picture is a unified image of horizontal stripes, a great square of them, alternating between pitch blackness and the brownish gray that rises just as night exhausts itself. This regimentation has the sureness of one who is devoted, who has an answer. The touch is absolutely cool. The hand has withdrawn. Of course, the picture being done when it was, in 1979, is properly Minimalist, adhering to the hands-off look of the style. Still, I'm imagining the romantic story: the painting's low vibration is the lover's austere declaration, tired after a long night of talk, reduced to one word of affirmation, whole in itself because in it the lover finds himself, like this simple image, unified with the beloved. His desire is satisfied by uttering it. It joins them. All he need do now is say it: *Catherine*.

For the lovers, wholeness is their goal. To become one with the other, completed. It's an old aspiration. Aristophanes, in Plato's dialogue about love, the *Symposium*, tells the fantastic story of the hermaphrodite. These bizarre beings were half male, half female, rolled together as one, globular creatures with four legs, four arms, and so on. But when the god Zeus became angry, he cut them down the middle, sliced like an egg, Aristophanes says. Forever after, the male has yearned for the female. The one side desperate to be joined once again to the other.

The story is not so different, really, from Eve taken from a rib of Adam. Or, for that matter, as St. Thomas Aquinas says, that "many men are derived from Adam, as members of one body." It's the dismemberment that brings us grief; the falling into sin from the goodness of the entire being. We are expelled from the dream of the universal into the fact of the particular, the individual self, our loneliness. "Mankind," Aristophanes says, "has never had any conception of the power of Love." So we are like pieces of coins, he says. The kind that children break in two for keepsakes.

Now Scully has spoken his lover's name. He has made the picture, inscribed it with the invocation of love. In the first instance, he gives us their union. The lovers are married in this conjugation of stripes. I imagine them as these signs, perfectly unified in the square, all sides being equal. But the story continues, another chapter. By the next year, something has been added, just as something has been taken away. The image is split, the geometry of the relationship is no longer of completely equal measures. The rectangle describes a square that has been altered, cut into matching lengths. And here it is sliced down the middle like Plato's sad hermaphrodite. Nothing is the same. The left side is still a night-lit image, but the stripes now run in strict verticals. To the right, the picture shifts. It moderates toward light. The stripes don't follow either. They move in the opposite direction, from side to side.

The picture is all about difference, the whole divided, about parts. There are two voices opposing. The halves are like two people forced into a narrow space. It is suffocating; it's as if they try to turn away from each other. Yet they are still joined—even made from the same matter, even sharing black as an element of their identities, even painted in the same way. All the black stripes, horizontal and vertical, are brushed in small, rising strokes.

Is it, then, that they're not as they seemed? After some small sleep, they are turning toward each other. The light is coming up. They know that love is more difficult than the first utterance of its name. It's only the second picture. This declaration of love has hardly started. The flush of hope, of the dream of wholeness, is like the prayer said at the beginning of the feast. Now the light is breaking, showing them the fallen world they had forgotten only for an instant, and the picture wakes to the truth of parts.

The pattern is natural enough: the lovers are intoxicated, they lose themselves in each other. Then time passes. They realize that even if they stay together, they have to get on with their own lives. After all, they're still pieces, individuals. A complexity grows. How can they hold on to their sense of oneness when they're split down the middle? But they accommodate. Love demands it. Love, Socrates says later in the *Symposium*, is the child of Need and Resourceful-ness. It's always hungry, yet it finds a way. And so the sense of partness isn't only about things fallen into separateness but about a desire to embrace the other element, to regather a lost unity. That is the balm of art. To mold whole-ness from divided parts.

The story takes on a radiance. True, Scully breaks up his next picture so clearly that the image, at first, seems abrupt, out of balance, disjointed. But one part is as strong as the other. The gray bands of the little panel seem to draw their power from the painting's stripes, as if the smaller area had accumulated an extra density, a weight equal to the rest of the picture. It is 1981, and the lovers have survived into a light very much like morning. For all the brightness of the yellow, there is an airy calm. The white bands are as pale as a clock face, and the parts move together, joined by the rhythmic marks of the brush, with all the constancy of a clock's hands.

The next year's work is really no different. It is only more intense. The color has become incandescent. The red glows, the orange no less. The inset of cool, contrasting blues is moved to the center, and the left side of the picture is lower, notched down, as if to heighten this thought that the separateness of parts only augments the power of their union. Arthur Schopenhauer, the 19th-century German philosopher, in speaking of love in *The World as Will and Idea*, writes: "Now the more perfect is the mutual adaptation of two individuals to each other . . . , the stronger will be their mutual passion."

The passion of these paintings, as they appear year after year, is about constancy. Of course, this is a formal passion, an obsession with making a certain kind of picture. The stripes expand and contract. They're combined, adapted to work in opposition, endlessly expressing a range of emotions, drawing the parts together. But in the story of the "Catherine" paintings, the passion and constancy also describe love, declaring devotion.

The paintings are a gift, they speak to the beloved. The gift is about absence—*Though I'm not there*—and affirmation—*Though I'm not there, I love you*. The pathos of the gift is its reminder of their separation, this distance between lover and beloved. It calls out, attempting to overcome their incompleteness. Through the gift, the lover draws near. He insinuates intimacy, dreaming of union, imagining wholeness.

Now the paintings seem to step forward; they become bodily. They're painted with a broader brush. The paint itself is thick, heavy, lustrous. The pigment glistens in great brushy passages, suspended in the oil, capturing light. The pictures, though large before, take on the mass of architecture, with panels jutting out into space, overhangs like lintels, planks as stout as columns or standing figures. They've given up their Minimalist cool. The passion is overt. The magisterial precision of those early stripes, done with masking tape, has given way to a literal pouring forth of the painter's body, his arm and hand rising freely through the currents of his feelings.

The range of his emotional life is like a garden accumulating varieties. It's expressed through the laying on of colors. Each year the variety grows in richness. The combinations, the layers, the muted tones and bright blasts acquire a new magisterial edge that replaces the austereness of his sentiments in those first dark paintings with this lavish unfolding. Distance is replaced by vulnerability. The flesh-colored bottom panel in "Catherine," 1983, is like an opening into softness, the lovers' bodies at rest in shadows. The immense somberness of the black-and-blue canvas, done the following year, is a bristling struggle, a war of melancholy against the broken-up, brilliant pieces of orange and black to its left.

The images are now about exposure, about the chances one takes on the field of emotions. Constancy is now visibly earned. The parts become more numerous. The proportions of the paintings are physically overpowering, as if the attempt to adapt these pieces to one another, to create a satisfying whole, has become difficult and awkward. The gift calls out with the promise of intimacy, yet it towers over the beloved. Its marker imposes. It says, too ominously, *I am always here*. There's something monstrous about it, isn't there? This domination, it's more about love of himself than of her.

Still, Scully's ability to express this gamut, to unveil this humanness, is impressive, touching. He says, *Look at my weakness, anger, my trust, my will to possess. My goodness includes my failings. All of it is here in the moods and*

*ambitions of these paintings. It's here that I say, "This is how I love, in my being.
This is my love, for you."*

Now, as you're reading this, perhaps you're thinking this is really too
much. This content—love, possession—where does it come from? After all,
these are stripes, panels, a series of abstract pictures—if they're impressive, it's
the sheer size of them, the palpable force of the brushwork, which is almost
brutal. You can see the paint dragged across these enormous surfaces, and the
physicality of that, as opposed to the refinement of most paintings or the size of
most paintings, is like a spectacle, like a theater for the eye. The eye roams
around, it registers the phenomenon. Then it turns away.

The presence of these unpeopled images raises the old question, What are
they for? But abstract pictures have been around for nearly a century, long
enough that we merely shrug, having gotten used to the idea, and answer, because someone thought of them. Or, having thought some more, because the act
of painting, without referring to anything outside of itself, is meant to be enough,
like someone praying in the street. It's a spiritual act, pushing aside the world.
It's not so much that the representation of the external world is exhausted as that
a new interest in the internal takes form. "Man turns his gaze away from the
external," Kandinsky says, "towards himself."

In some ways, though, it's not only personal, not only a hymn to the self.
It's like science, an empirical examination: Painting has gone deeper and deeper
into its own processes. After the long history of relatively realistic pictures came
Impressionism, which broke down the image of a field or of a sunset into
brushstrokes like light refracting. Then, in abstraction, everything else got
broken down too—landscapes, figures. Finally, the brushstroke itself or even the
canvas support on which it lies became the subject, the object of interest. If it
doesn't speak to the world, at least it's got its logic. It's for its mere thingness, to
make you acknowledge that there is a thing in the world that is simply there as
an object for thought—like a standard, like the atomic clock, hermetically sealed,
by which all the other clocks are set. It's irreducible.

That is why the painting is called abstract. But, of course, that's not
enough. Each abstract picture is different. They breathe in their own ways.
They're formed by different imaginations. And that is it, really—that we, the
viewers, need to create too. We project onto the abstraction something that
makes it local for us, real. Yes, we rob it of some of its mere thingness for our
own pleasure, our own needs.

That is why I'm imagining the story. I have been given the word
"Catherine." Have I been telling you about myself? It's true, I'm moved by the
idea of dedication, the declaration of love. It's a romantic story, isn't it? But one
that seems so much like life, with its difficulties, things broken up trying to find a

way through, something that's whole. And that's what I imagine here: the lover is wandering through himself, through her, finding a way. The ambiguities, the going back and forth of these stripes, the parts shifting directions, roughly or more smoothly painted, they're all part of it—teeming with ambivalence and passion, this aching constancy.

The years flood by. The paintings engage in this uneasy balancing act. One year, 1986, the picture is about heat and solitude, or, just as easily, about coldness and attraction. Dark blue, a shadowed red, and the edgy rectangle of blue and a gray finished with red, like steel piercing the heart, to the left. The next year, a new sympathy, an equilibrium, is obvious. The inset panels, though given stripes of opposite directions once again, are of equal size. They sit calmly on the same level. The painting itself is on a single plane, as if the gift is not about domination at all. It's a token, a light-filled reminder of domestic happiness. They are content.

And the pictures continue on—the parts abut, literally out of joint, assuaged by adjustments of blues and oranges and yellows, dipping into sadness, now raised up into the sun. They live in agitated harmony. That, in any case, is the economy of love. It may be, for example, that sometimes the gift for the beloved isn't even for the one he desires. But it's for the one with whom, despite eruptions and lapses, he has the habit of feeling whole. His constancy persists; the pictures become beads on a string. We watch an impulse that has led, through chance, reflection, and elaboration, to shapeliness.

The bodies I've conjured, the lovers in darkness and light; the panels drawing near or receding; the stripes and bands; the colors remote or forceful— they've all conspired to find in the other what's missing, what they lack and long for. The gift is the lover's longing; he implores through it, he cajoles, he hopes for his own completion. She is open, receptive. She turns away. Through their repetitions and variations, all of these relationships—of emotions, of parts, of brushwork—begin to take on a generality. It's as if their accumulating patterns speak of some other thing, underneath, being enacted. Just as Socrates' teacher suggests at the end of the *Symposium* "that lovers are people who are looking for their other halves, but as I see it, Socrates, love never longs for either the half or the whole of anything except the good." A map emerges, a shape spreads through the "Catherine" paintings—the vulnerability, the failures, pleasures, and devotion—of a deeper longing, an original union.

It's what Wordsworth talks about in his "Two-Part Prelude," the lines about the child nursed in his mother's arms: "Along his infant veins are interfused/The gravitation and the filial bond/Of Nature that connect him with the world." And Freud wonders at a friend's sense of an "oceanic feeling," a sensation of boundless oneness at the base of being human in *Civilization and its Discontents*, going on, like Wordsworth, to find its origin at the mother's breast.

Our separateness originates there too, he says, when the infant recognizes that the mother isn't a part of him. He's divided, an outside exists, the world is broken into parts.

So the paintings, as their patterns mount, become more than markers of erotic love. Scully passes something on, his picture of humanness: desire, sympathies, complications; people clasping, going off in anger, the pieces of the keepsake broken; coming back, the urge to continue. It's at last a moral picture, a moral tale. An idea emerges that beyond the specific limbs of personal love, there is precisely this love of our faulty, striving, sometimes satisfactory natures. The greater love is a love of our pathos, of seeing in our imperfections and aspirations the goodness of human will. And if, as Wordsworth says, we have a filial bond with Nature, then it's there, even beneath mother and child, that wholeness lies consummate and primal.

I imagine this in the last "Catherine" painting I've seen, the one from 1991, though others will follow, the story goes on. The canvas is reordered. The bands of the past are broken down still further into rectangles, checkers alternating in red and black. In the midst of them, two insets of stripes seem to float. The one at the top offers human reason, decisiveness—it's in dark blue and white, no and yes. The other is yellow and black, yellow of the sun and night. Culture and nature accommodate; they get along in the greater workings, in an endless complexity of parts. The lover and the beloved are there as well, divided yet equal, suspended in a world of fierceness, splashed out like a tumbler of fire and shadow.

Oh yes, I know that I'm reading this into the picture. There is a clear view from my window, a sky tinseled with clouds. I'm pulling these thoughts down into my study. They are not there in the painting exactly. They are not spelled out in a brightly lit narrative with figures and captions. It's only that the "Catherine" paintings have led me to think in a certain way, helped me to think. That is the hand they've offered, which my story opens.

THE CATHERINE PAINTINGS

Catherine, 1980
Oil on canvas
84 x 35 ½ inches (213 x 90 cm.) (two panels)

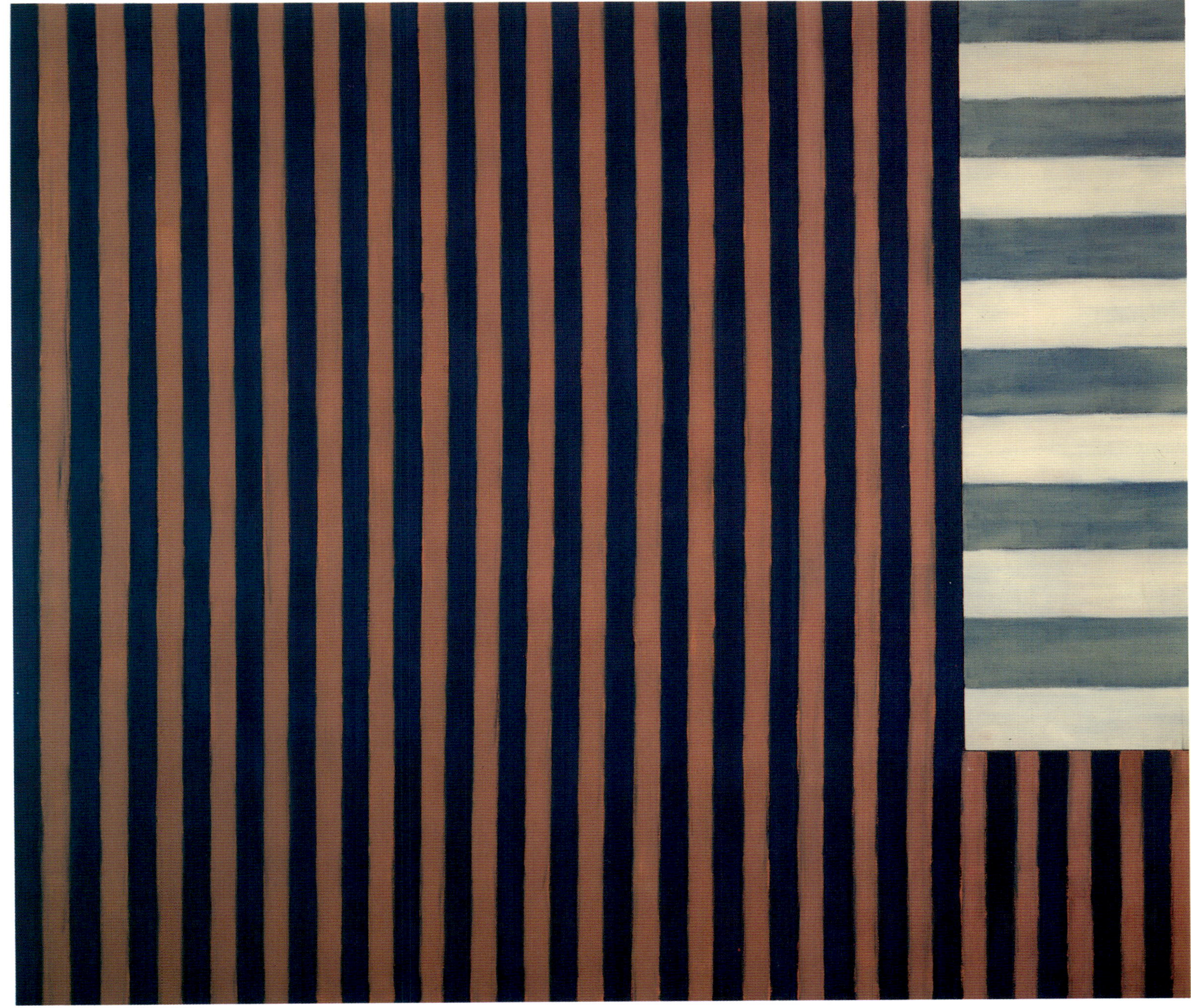

Catherine, 1982
Oil on canvas
114 x 97 ¾ inches (290 x 246 cm.)

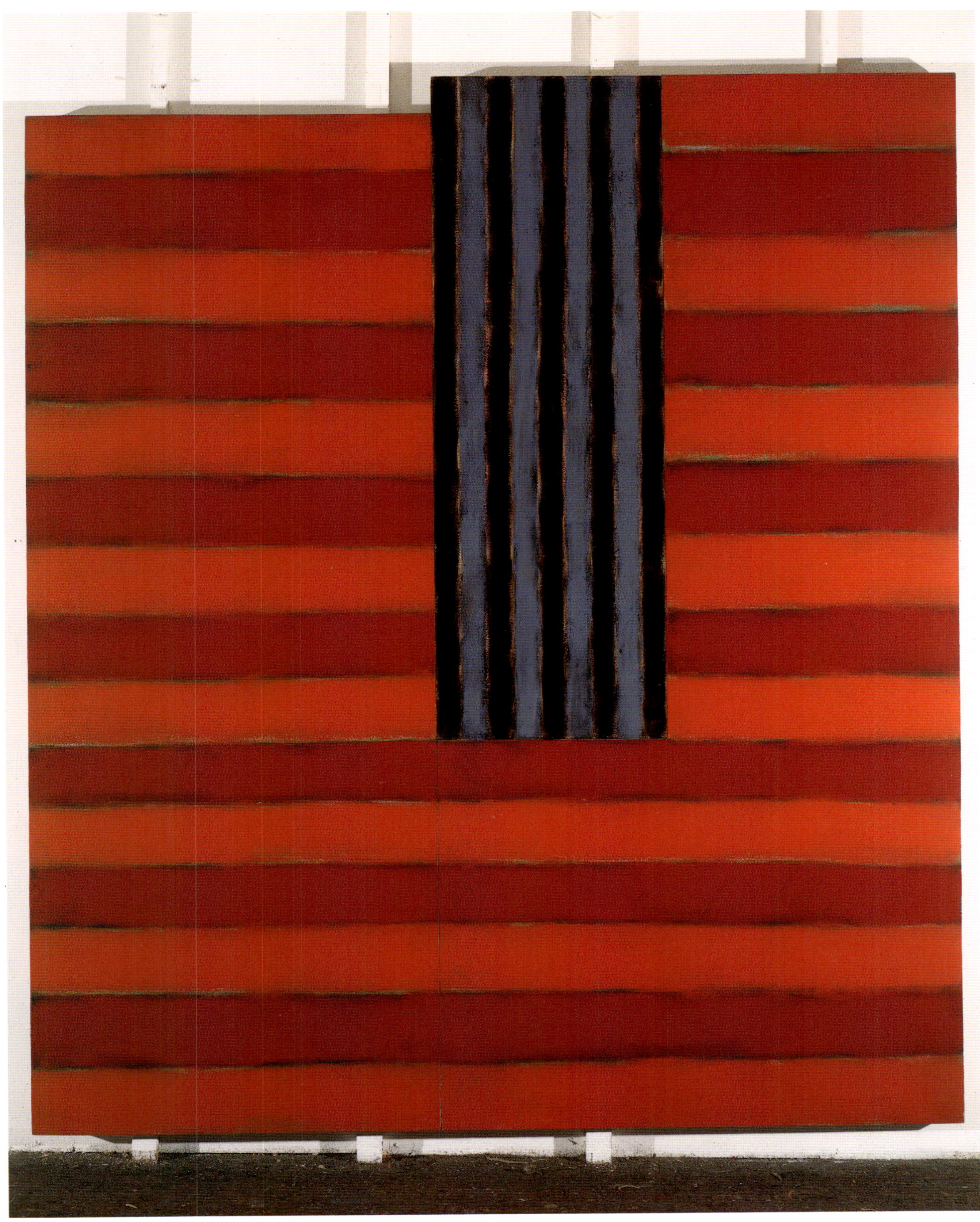

Catherine, 1983
Oil on canvas
116 x 96 inches (292 x 244 cm.) (two panels)

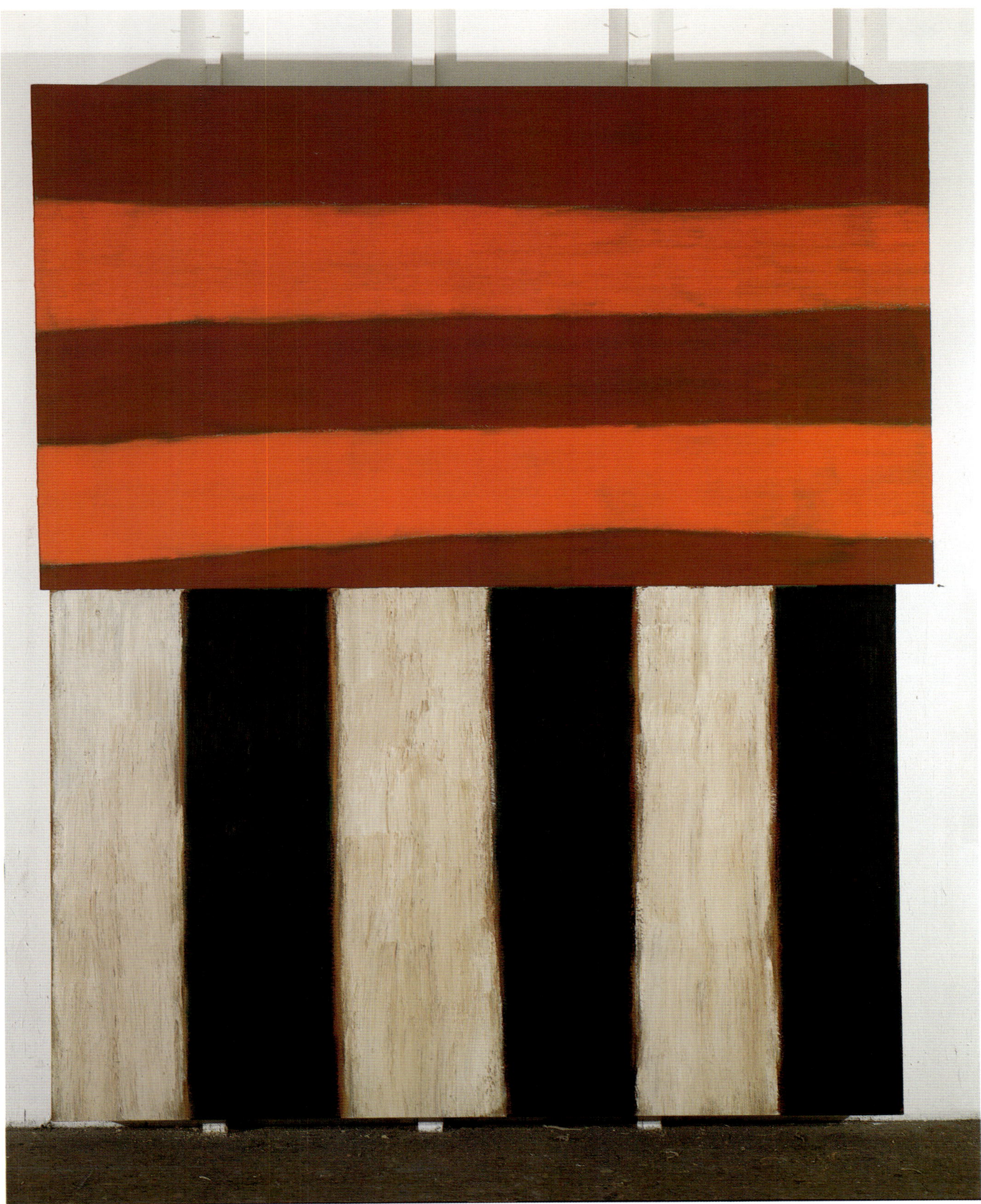

Catherine, 1984
Oil on canvas
102 inches x 134 inches (259 x 244 cm.) (three panels)

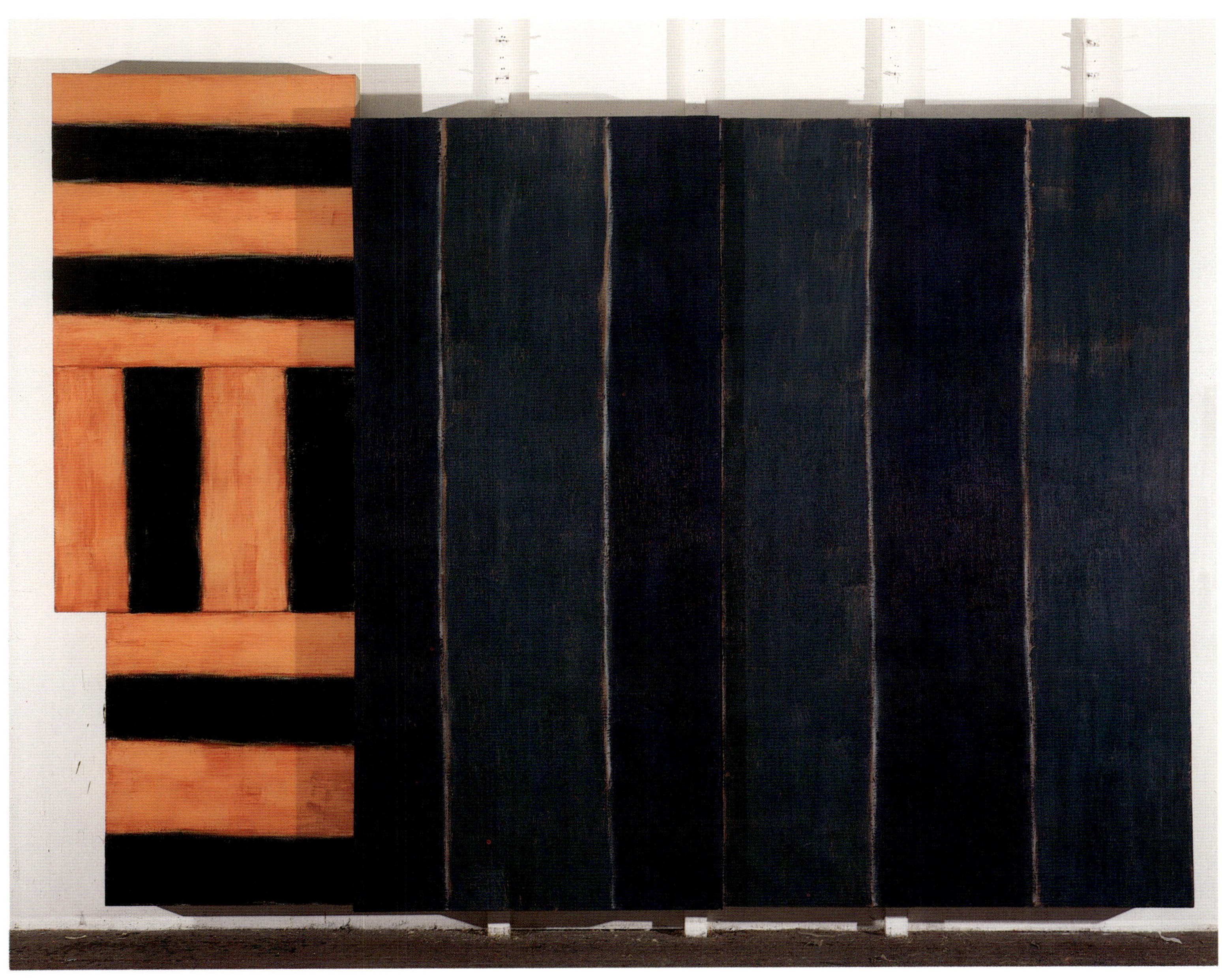

Catherine, 1985
Oil on canvas,
98 ½ x 99 ¼ inches (259 x 244 cm.) (two panels)

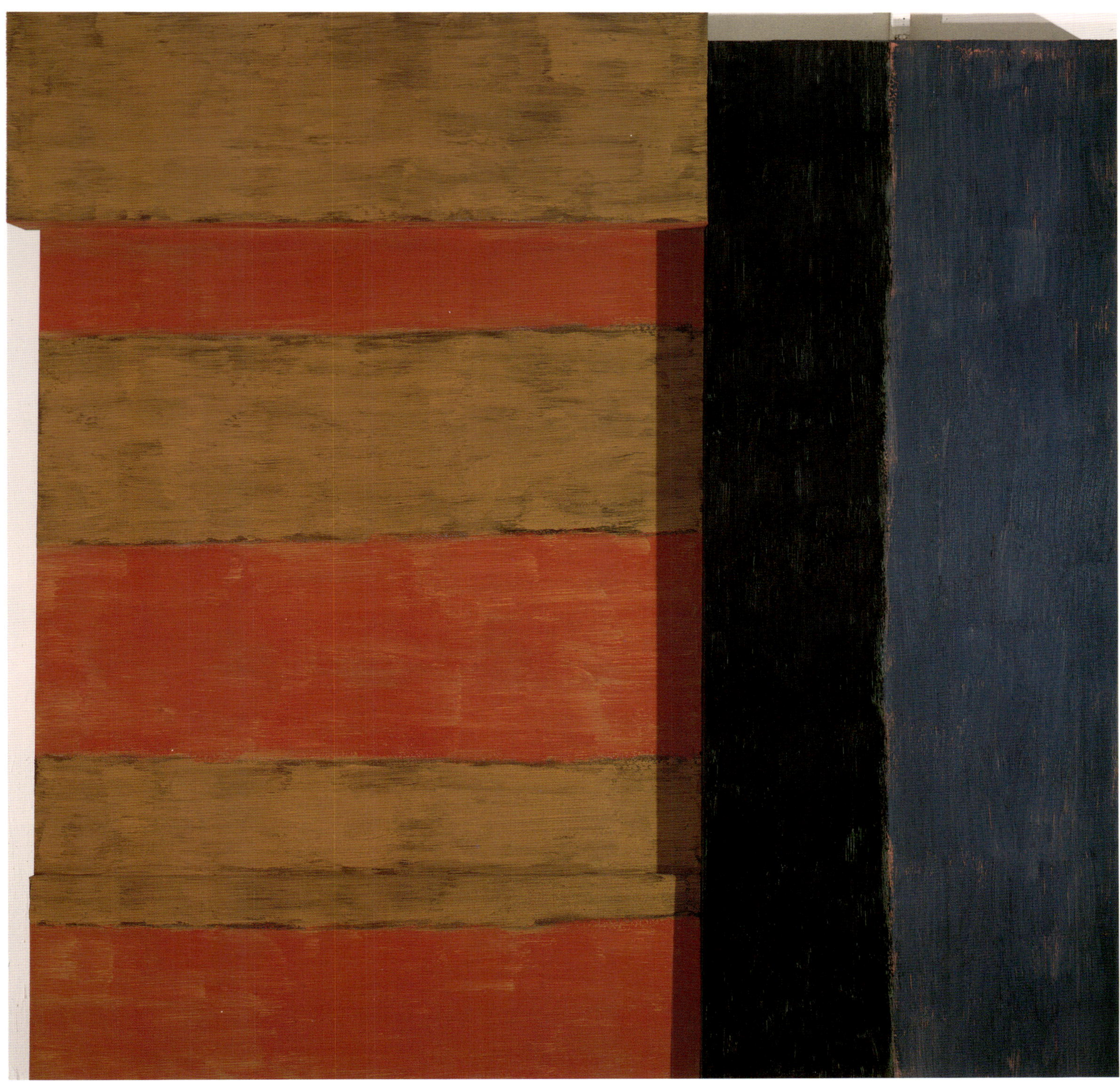

Catherine, 1986
Oil on canvas
96 x 132 inches (244 x 331 cm.) (three panels)

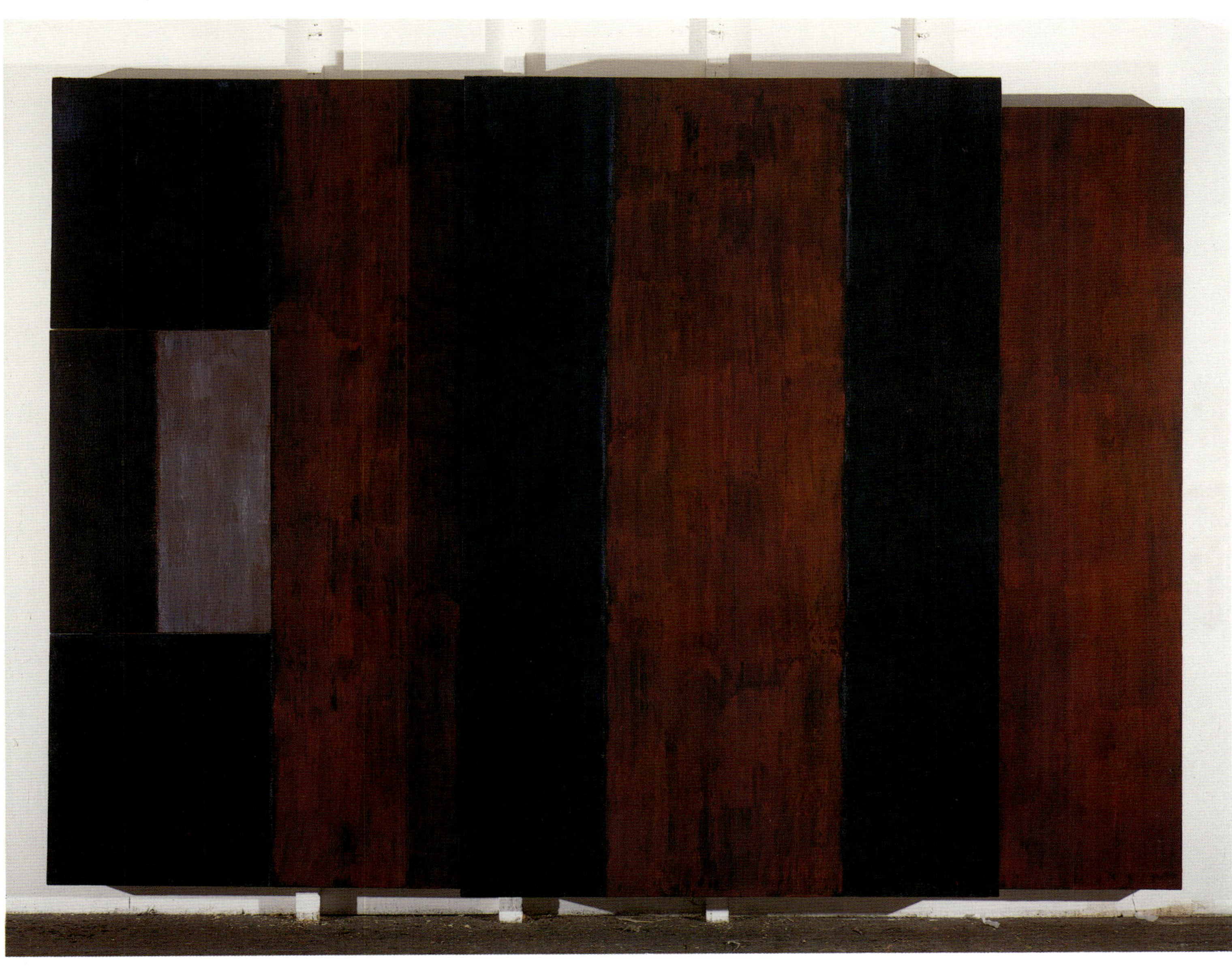

Catherine, 1987
Oil on canvas
96 x 120 inches (244 x 304 cm.) (two panels)

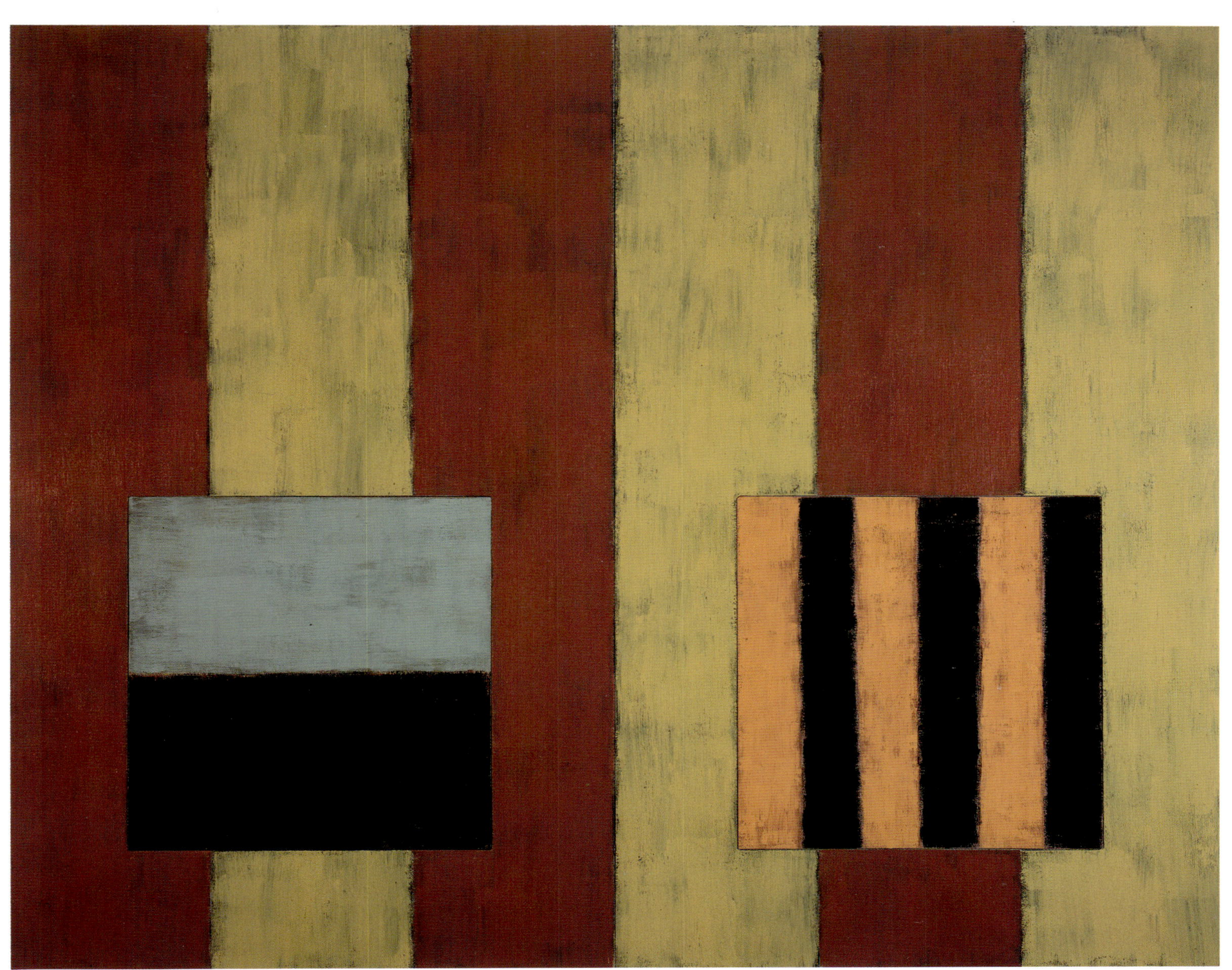

Catherine, 1988
Oil on canvas
100 x 120 inches (254 x 304 cm.) (two panels)

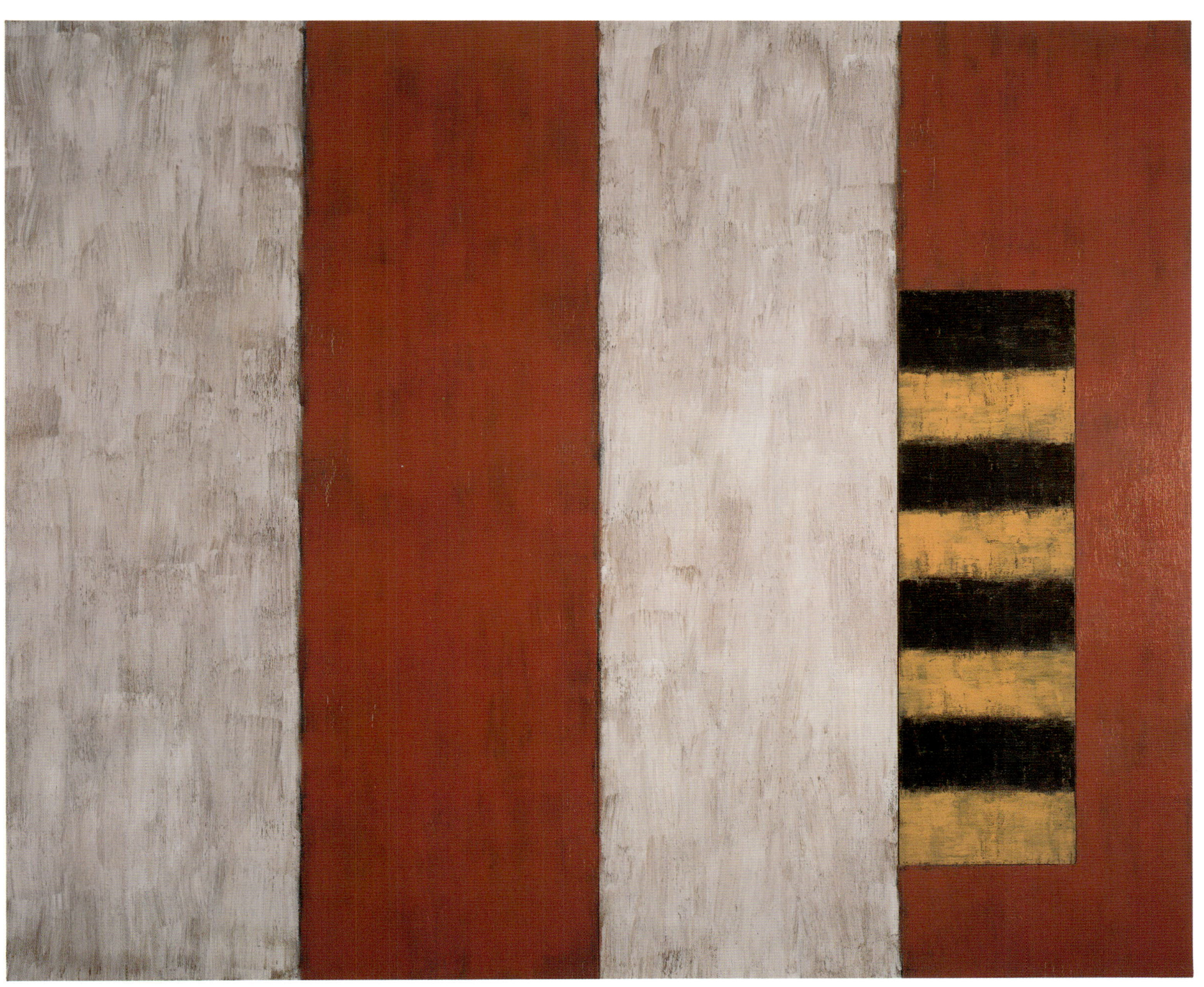

Catherine, 1989
Oil on canvas
102 inches x 136 inches (259 x 354 cm.) (two panels)

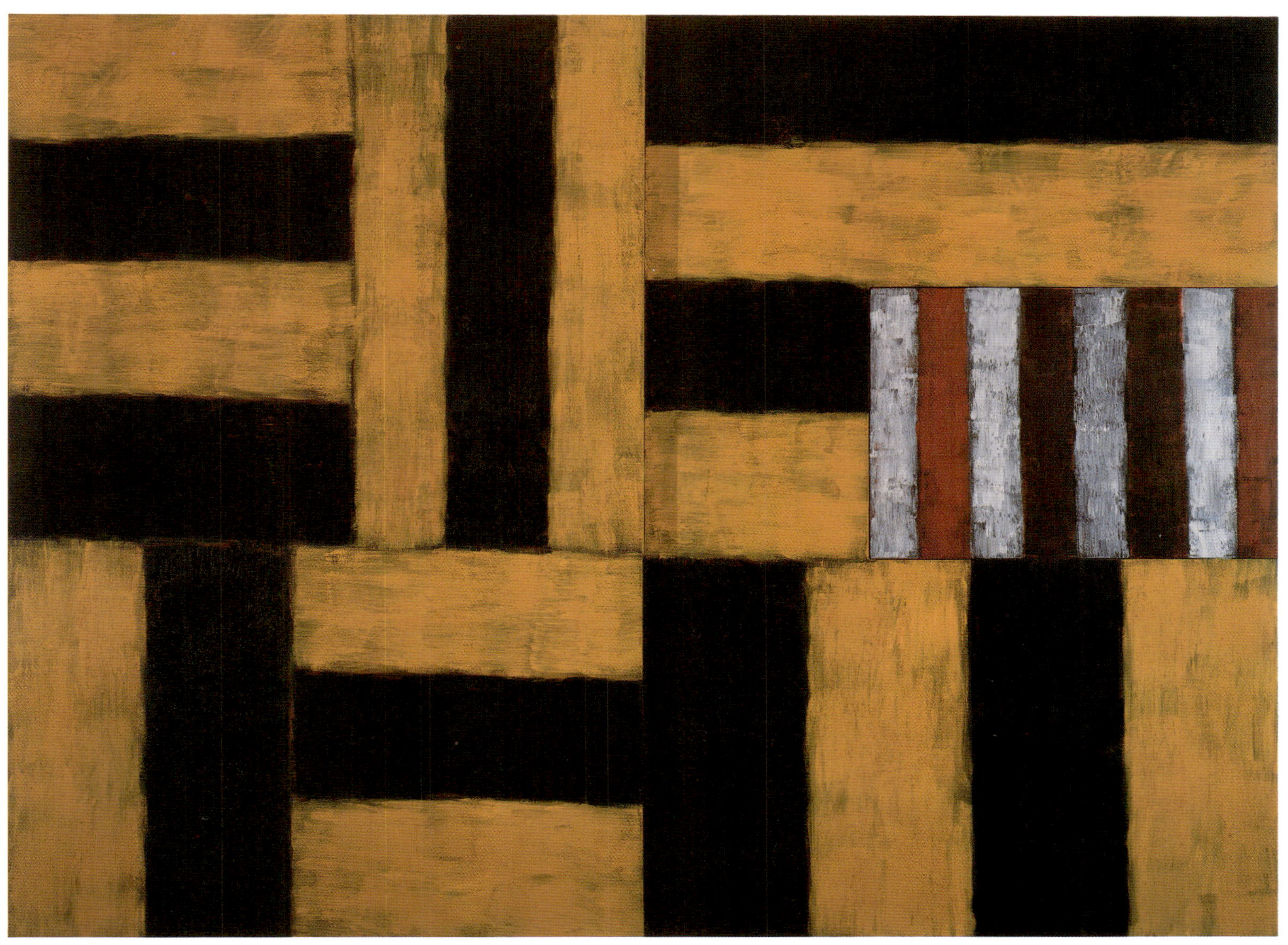

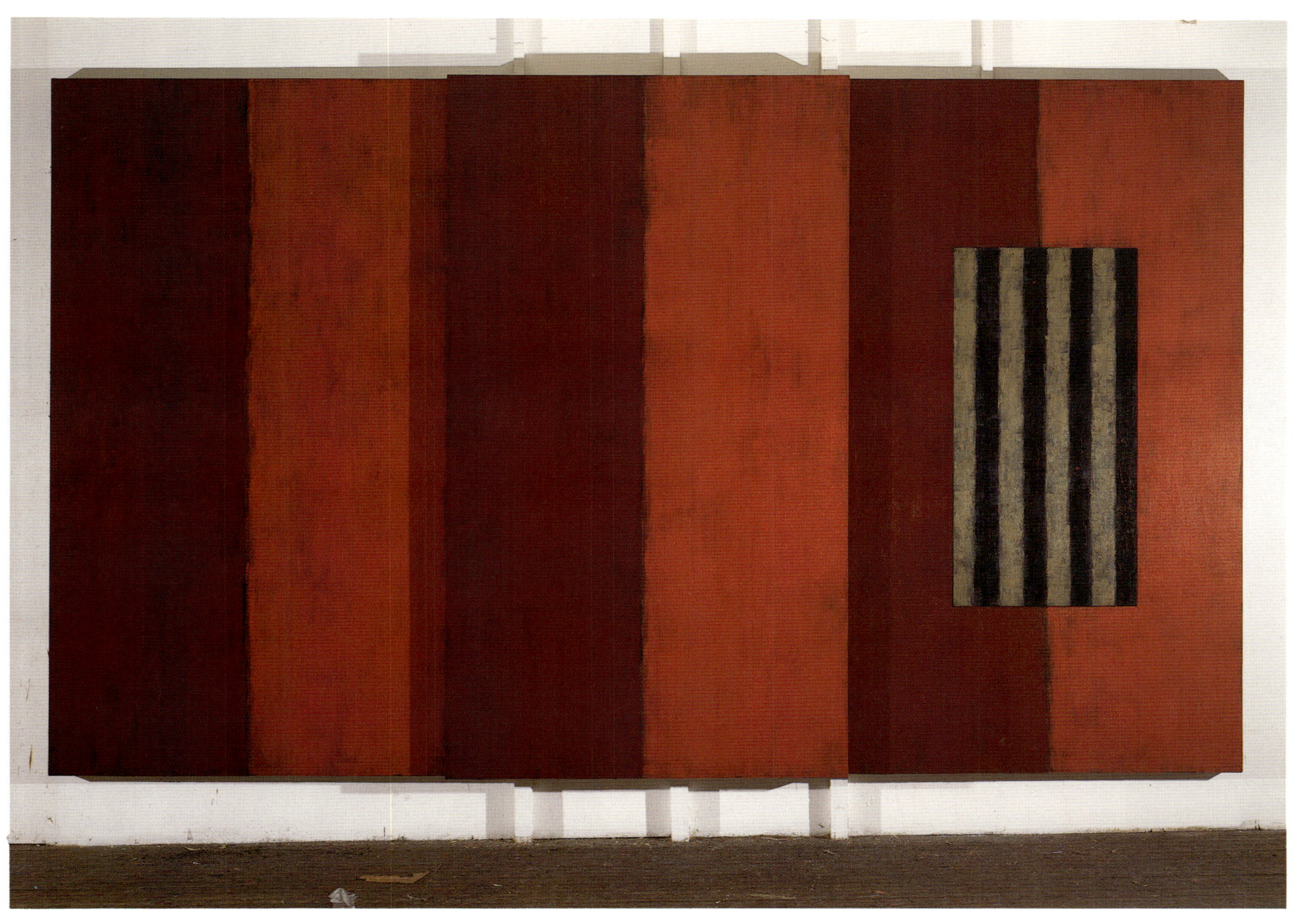

Catherine, 1991
Oil on canvas
100 x 88 inches (254 x 223 cm.) (two panels)

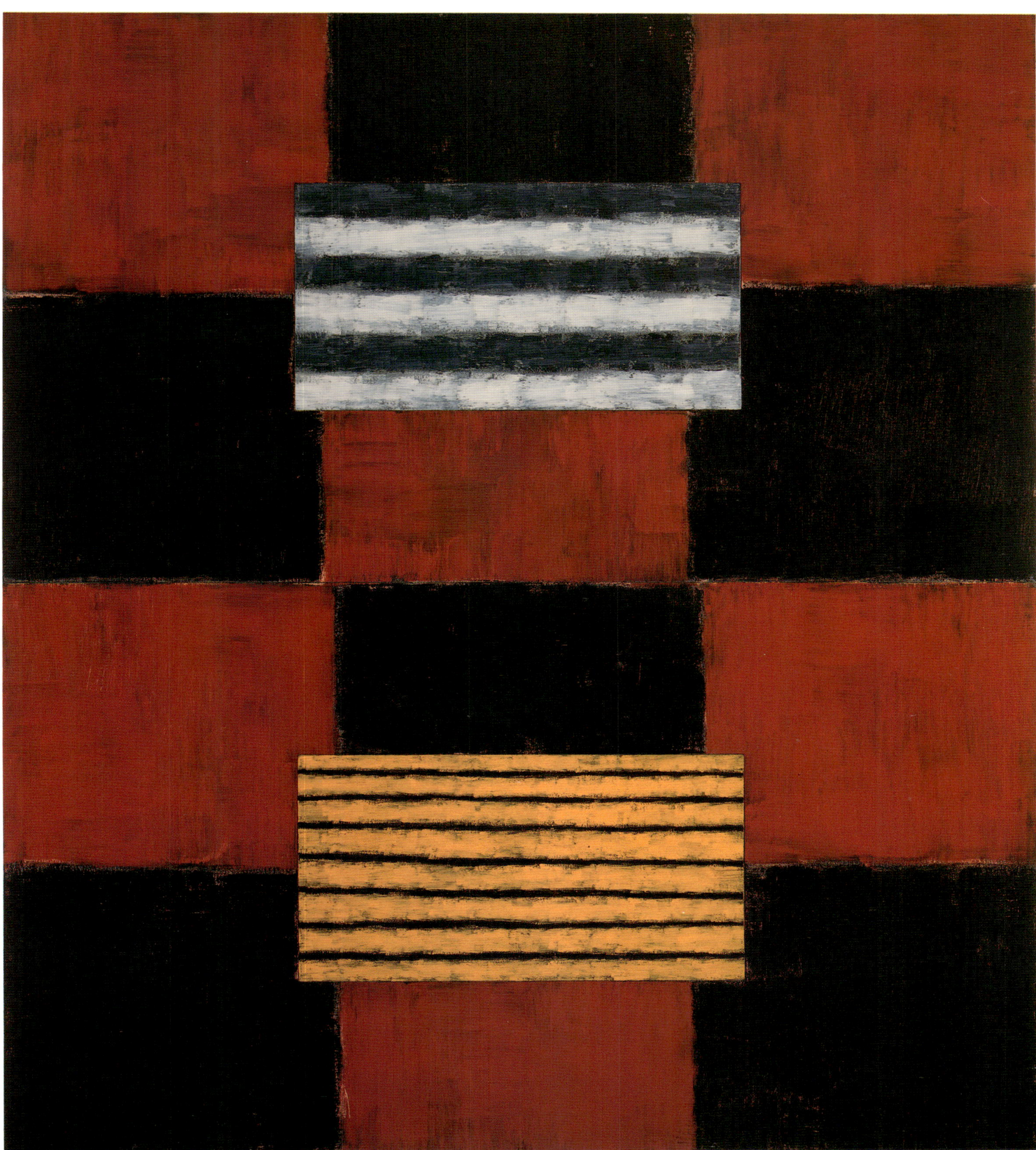

Catherine, 1992
Oil on canvas and metal
84 x 120 inches (213 x 305 cm.) (two panels)

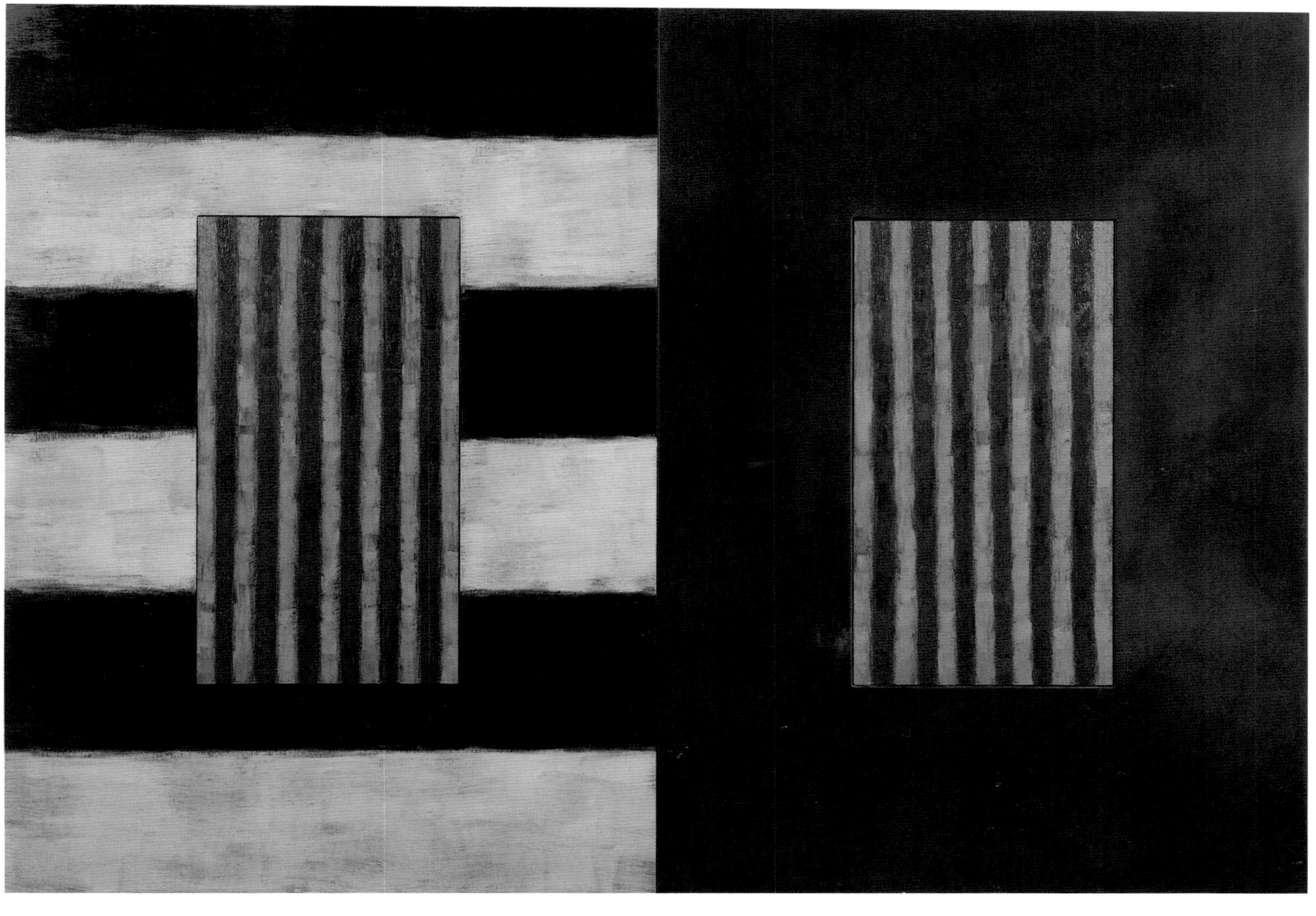

SELECTED WATERCOLORS

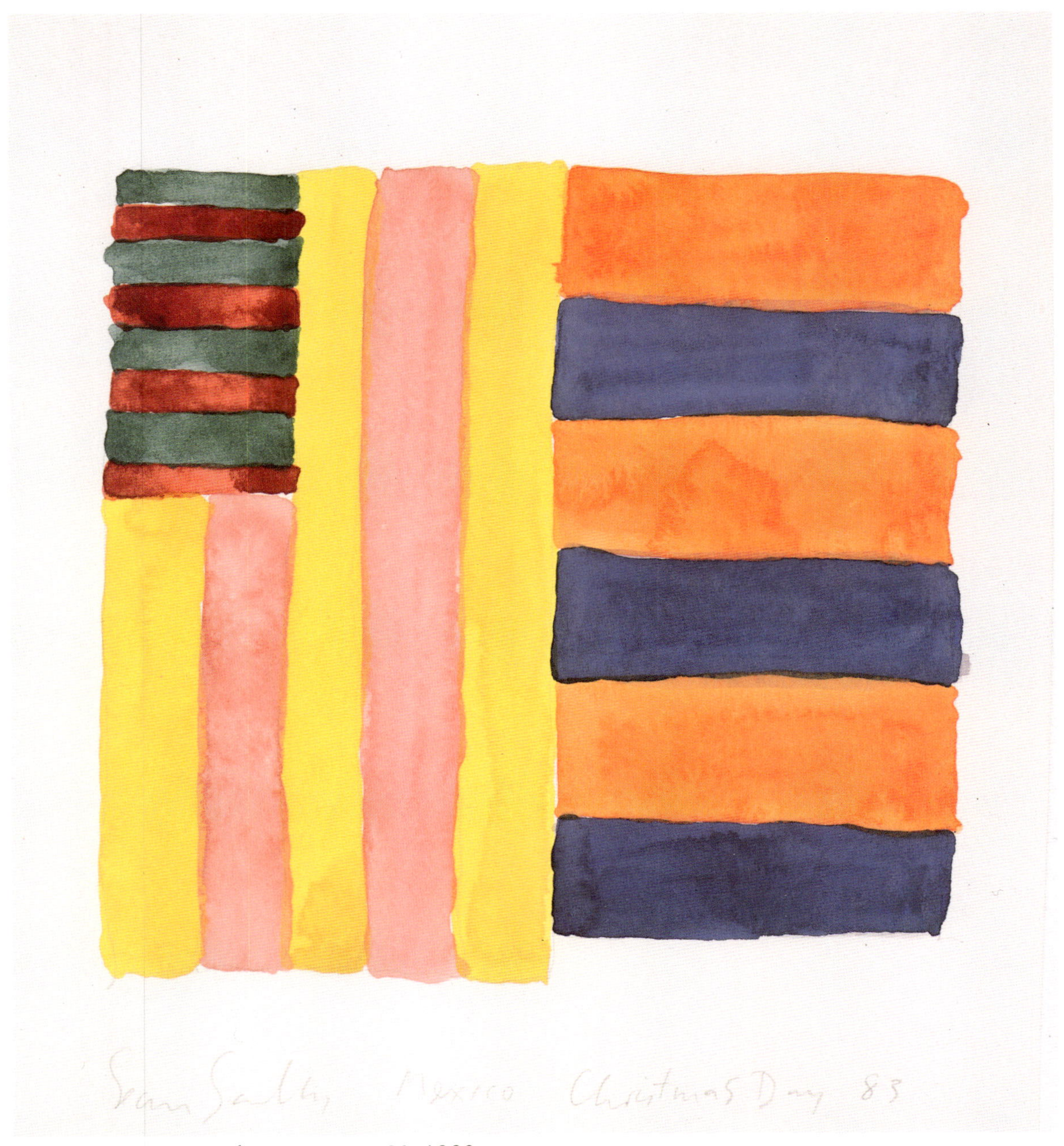

Cat. No. 2. *Mexico Christmas Day 83*, 1983

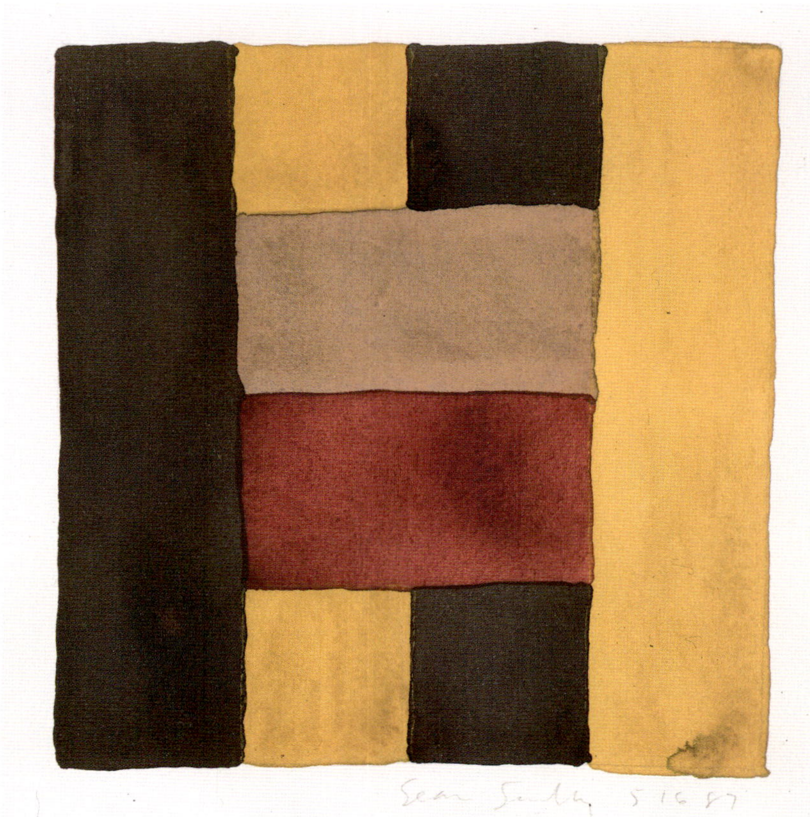

Cat. No. 14. *Untitled 5.16.87*, 1987

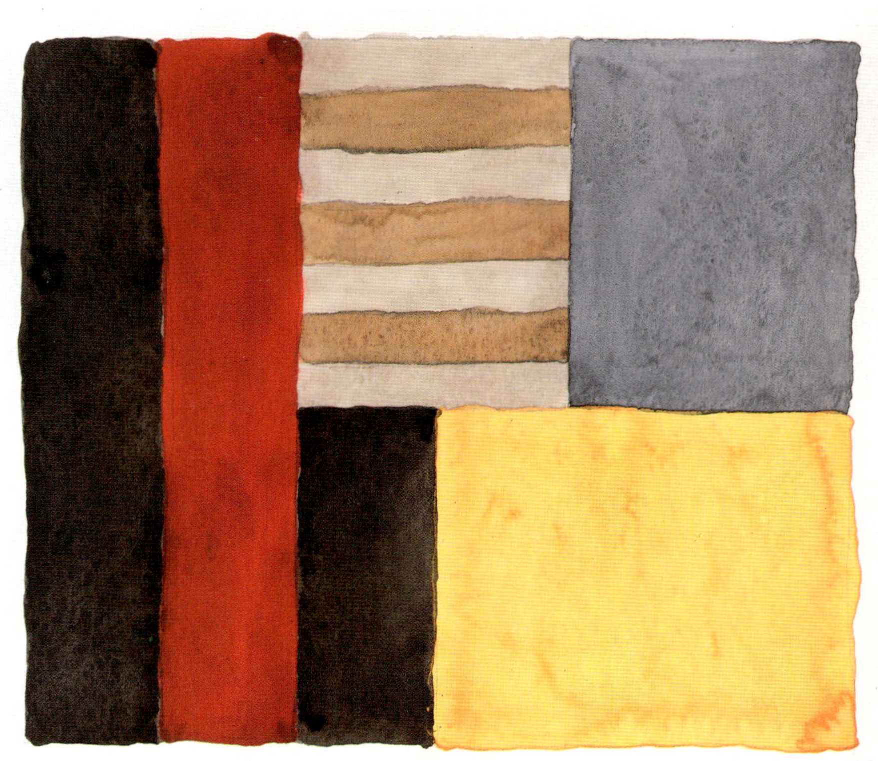

Cat. No. 19. *Untitled 10.26.87*, 1987

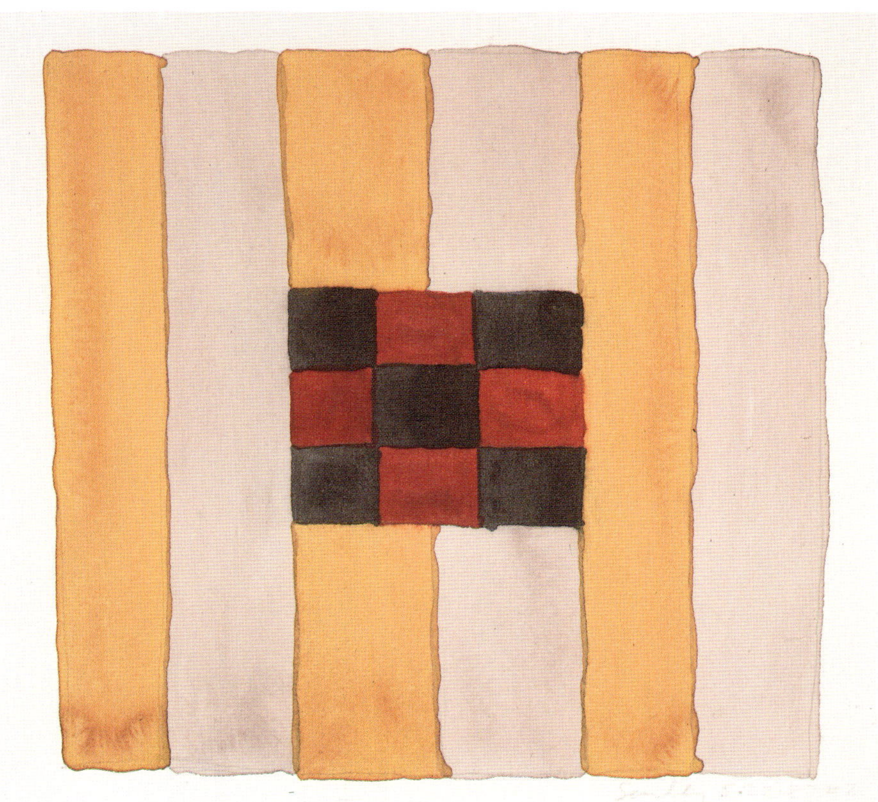

Cat. No. 15. *Untitled 5.22.87*, 1987

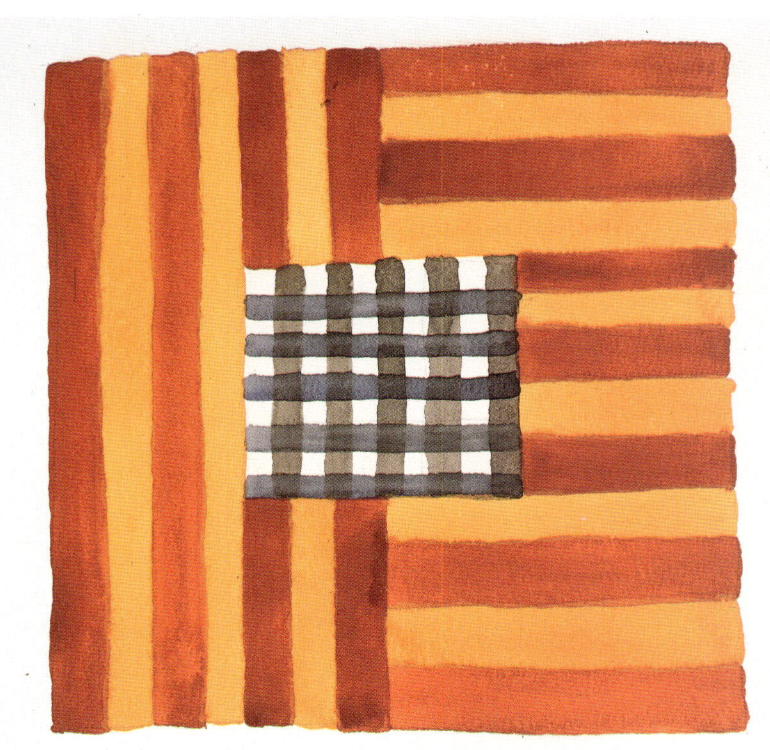

Cat. No.11. *Untitled 4.10.87*, 1987

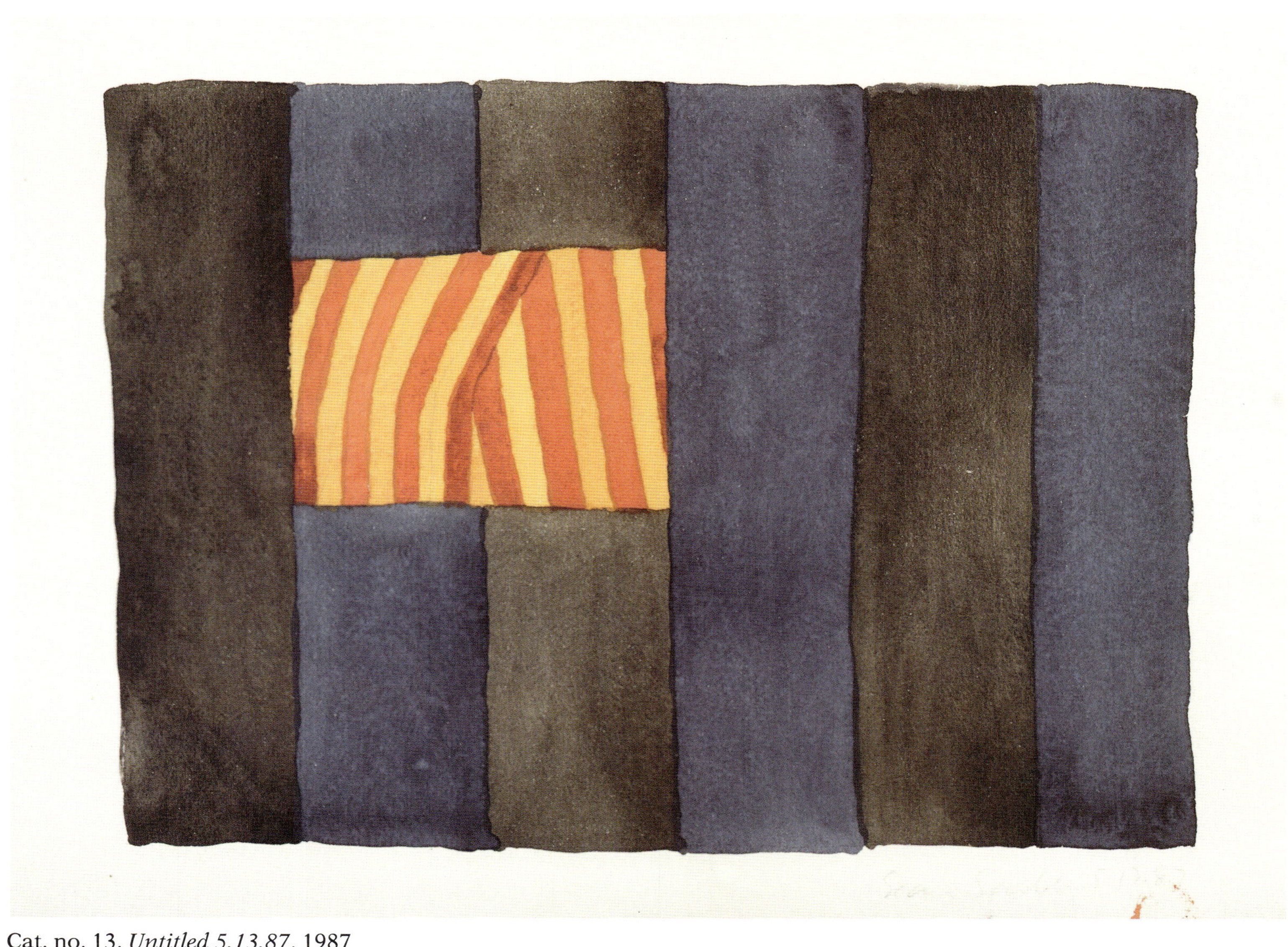

Cat. no. 13. *Untitled 5.13.87,* 1987

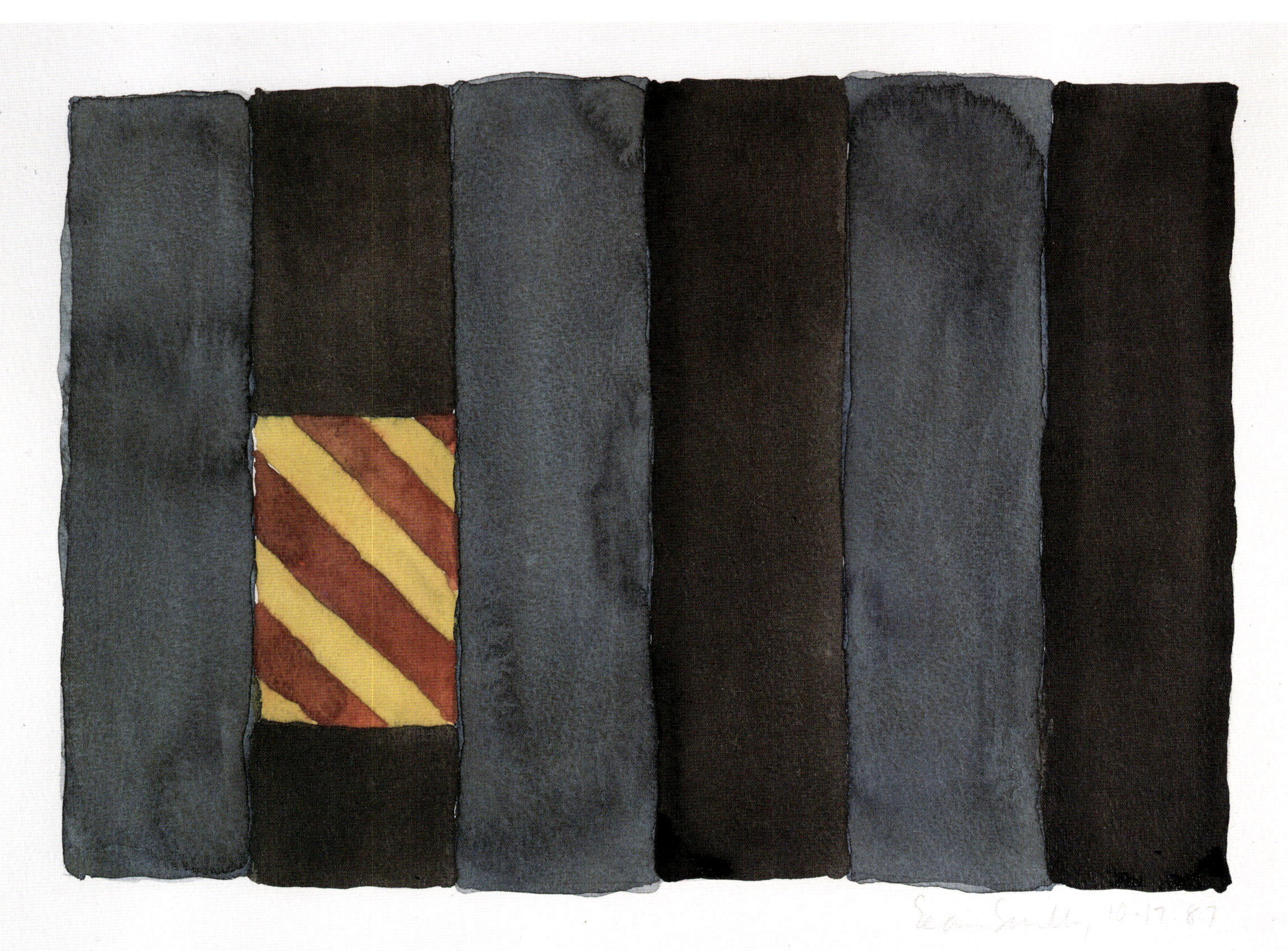

Cat. No. 18. *Untitled 10.17.87,* 1987

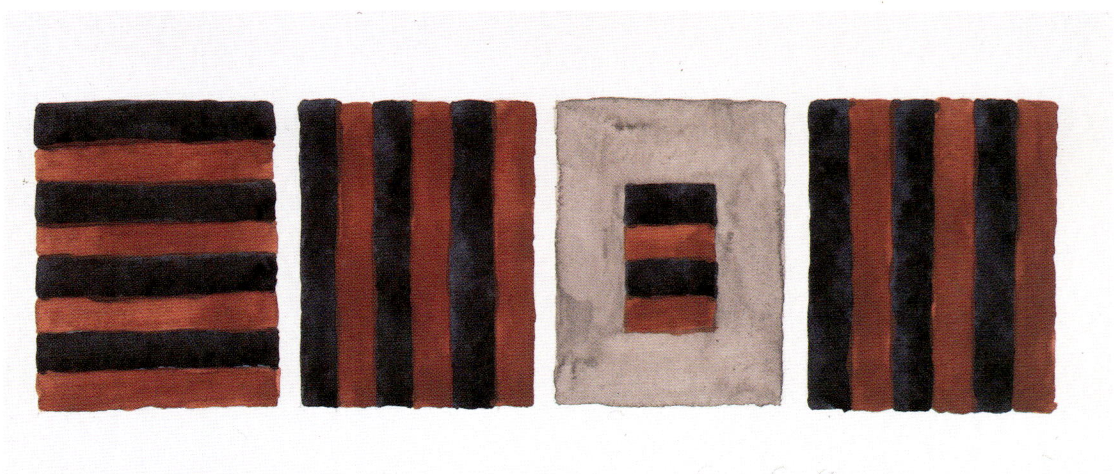

Cat. No. 22. *Untitled 2.20.90,* 1990

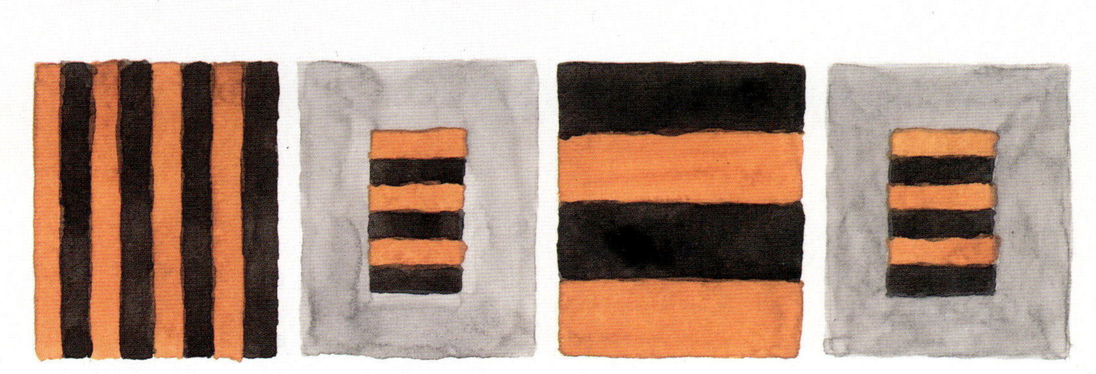

Cat. No. 23. *Untitled 2.24.90,* 1990

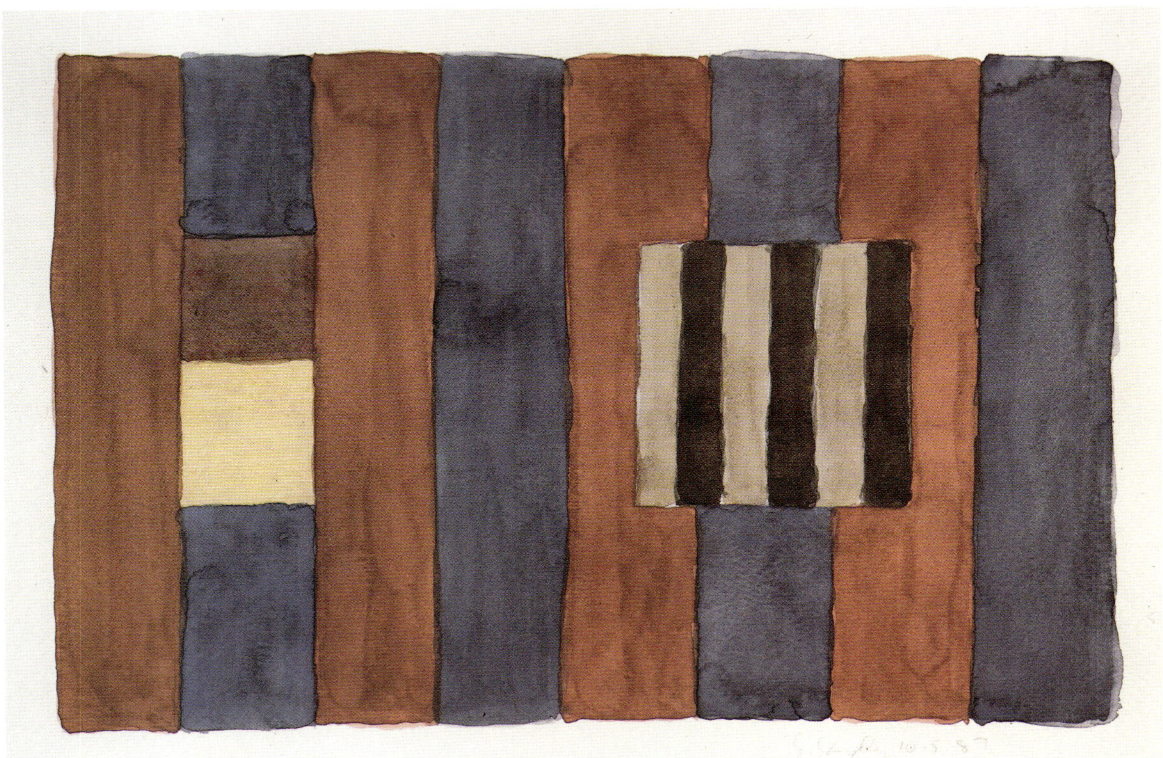

Cat. No. 17. *Untitled 10.5.87*, 1987

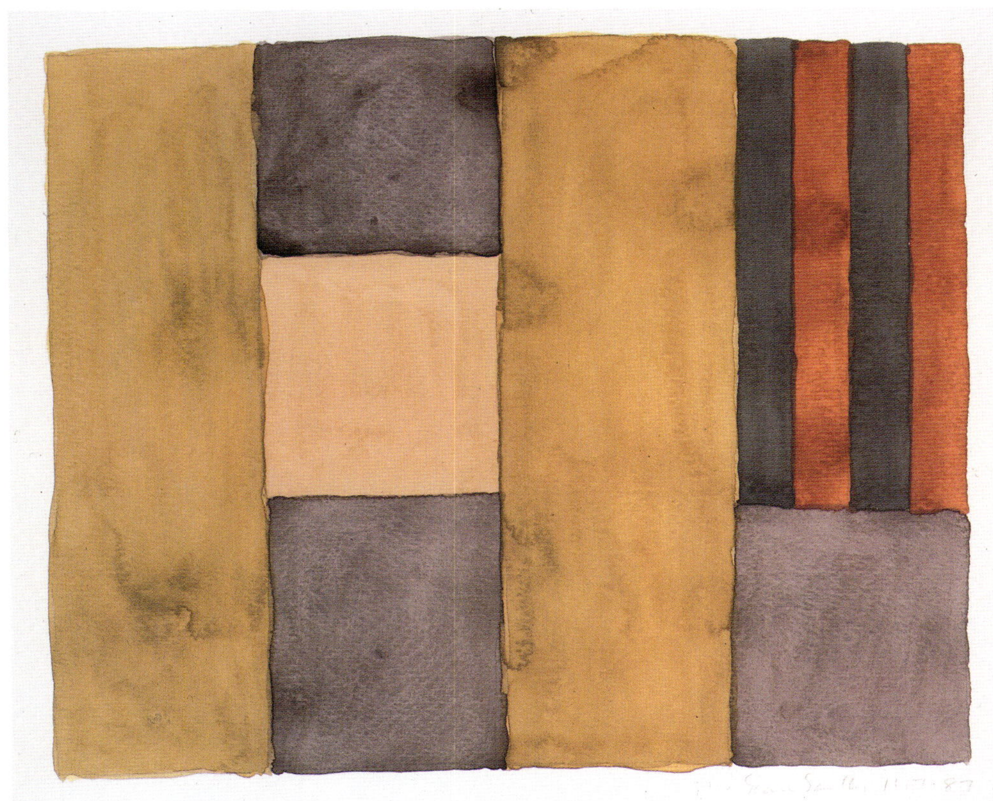

Cat. No. 21. *Untitled 11.7.87*, 1987

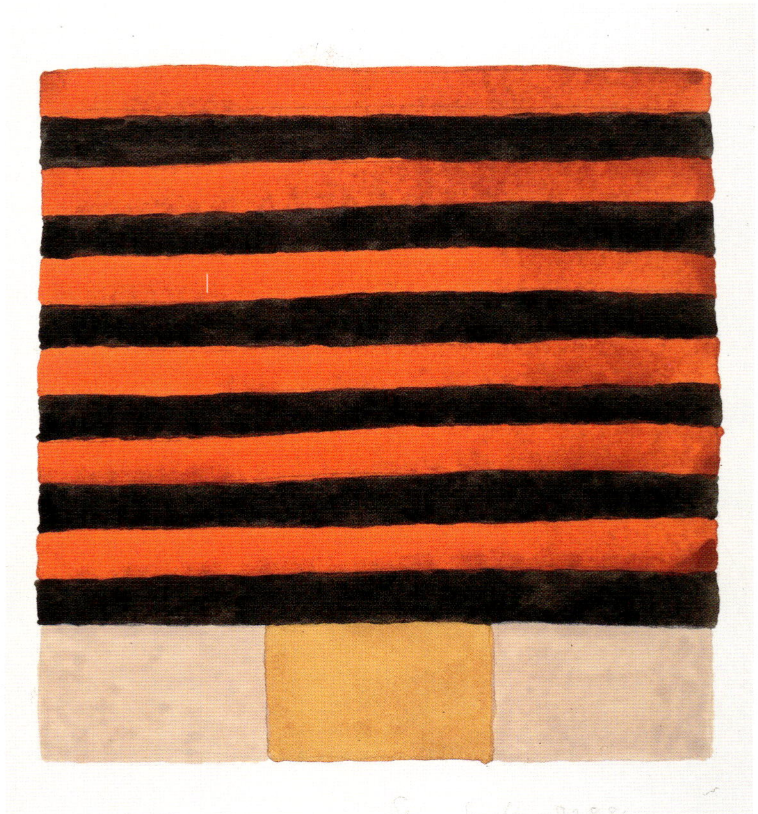

Cat. No. 9. *Untitled 8.28.86*, 1986

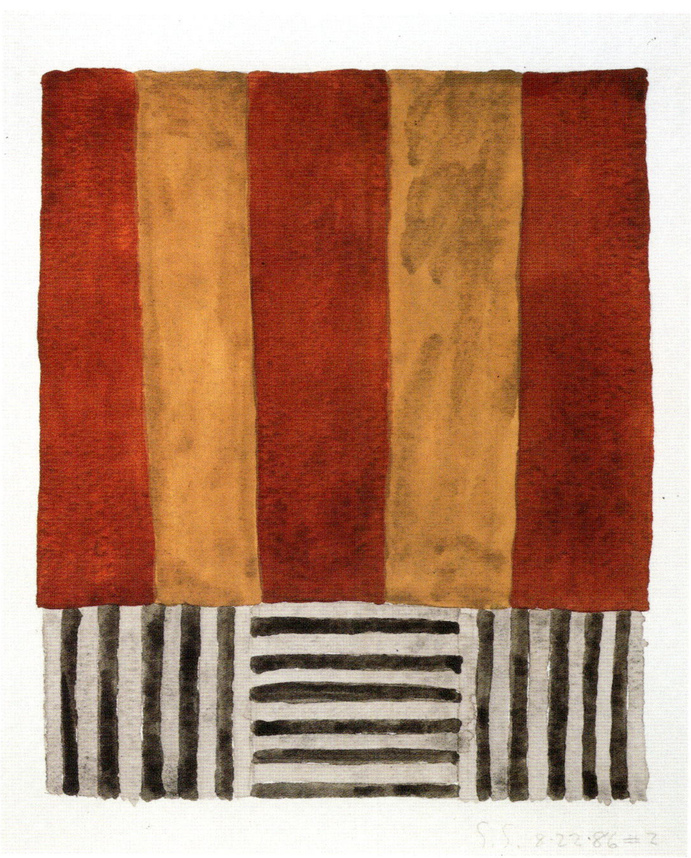

Cat. No. 8. *Untitled 8.22.86 #2*, 1986

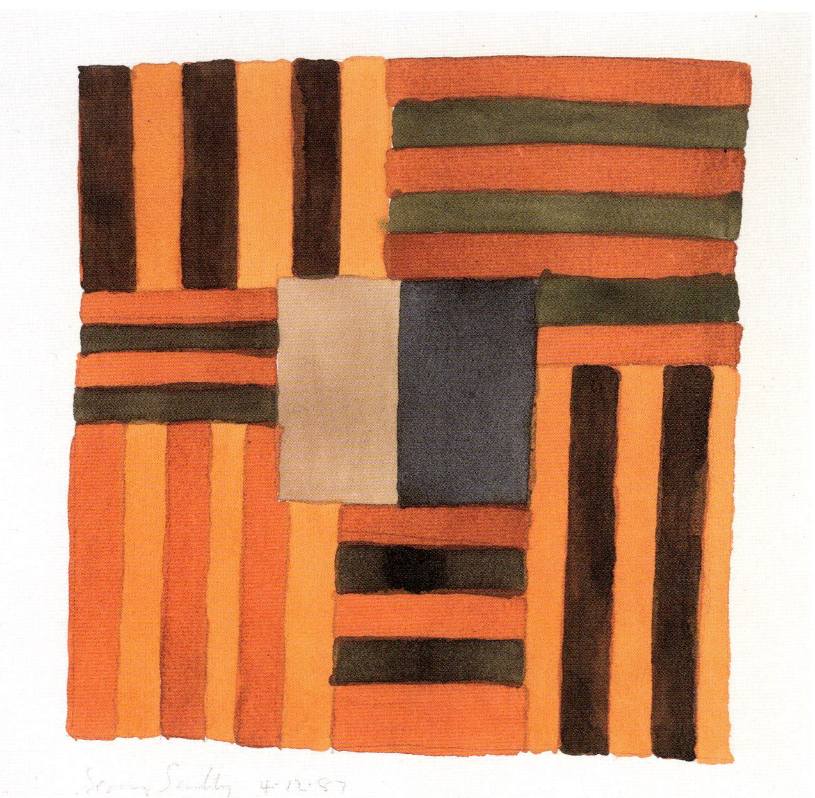

Cat. No. 12. *Untitled 4.12.87*, 1987

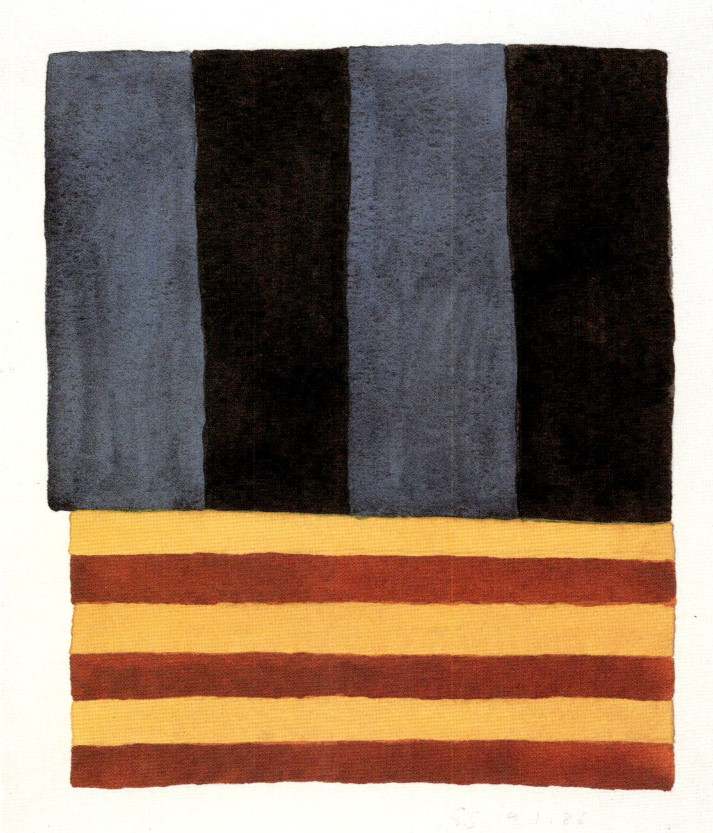

Cat. No. 10. *Untitled 9.1.86*, 1986

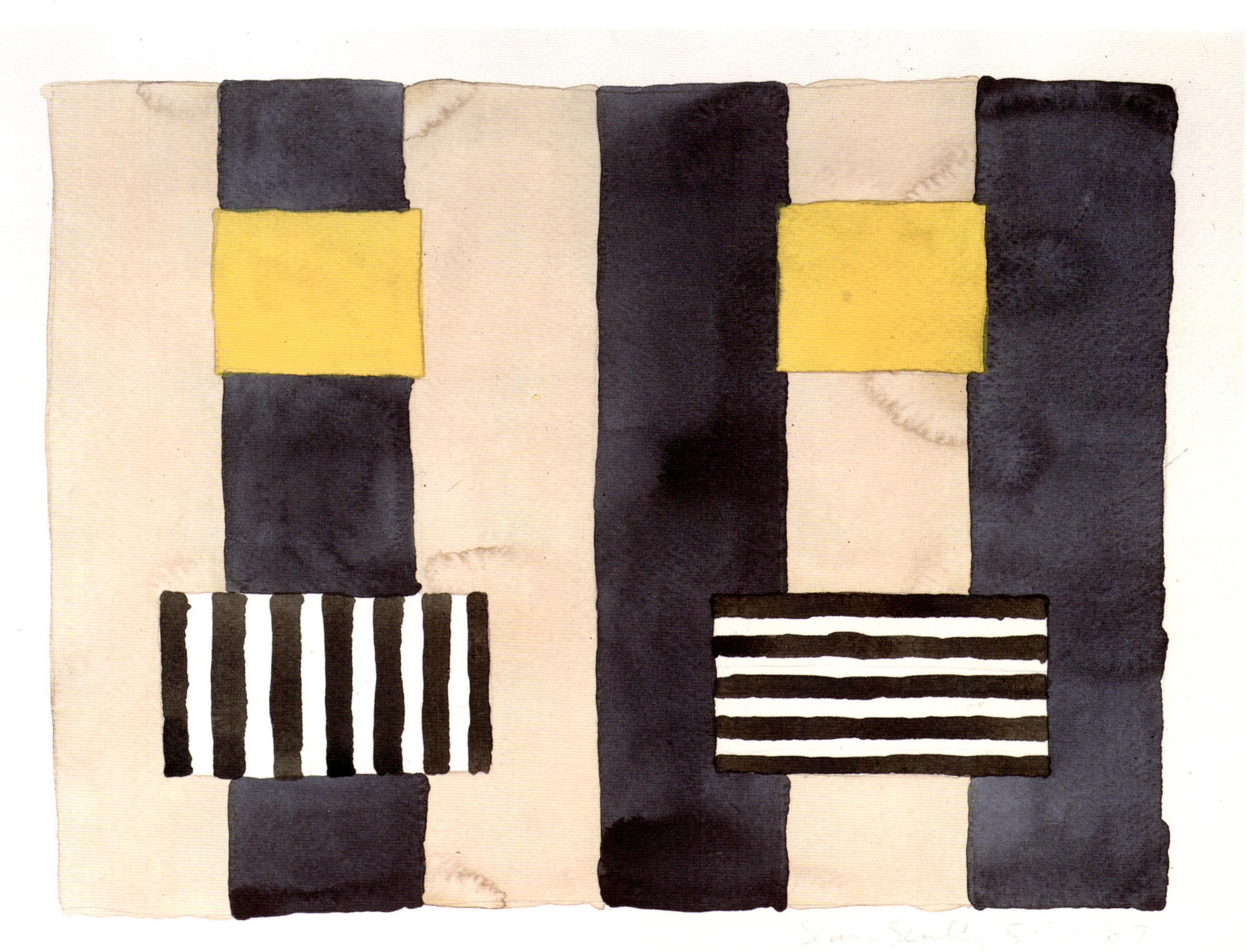

Cat. No. 16. *Untitled 5.31.87*, 1987

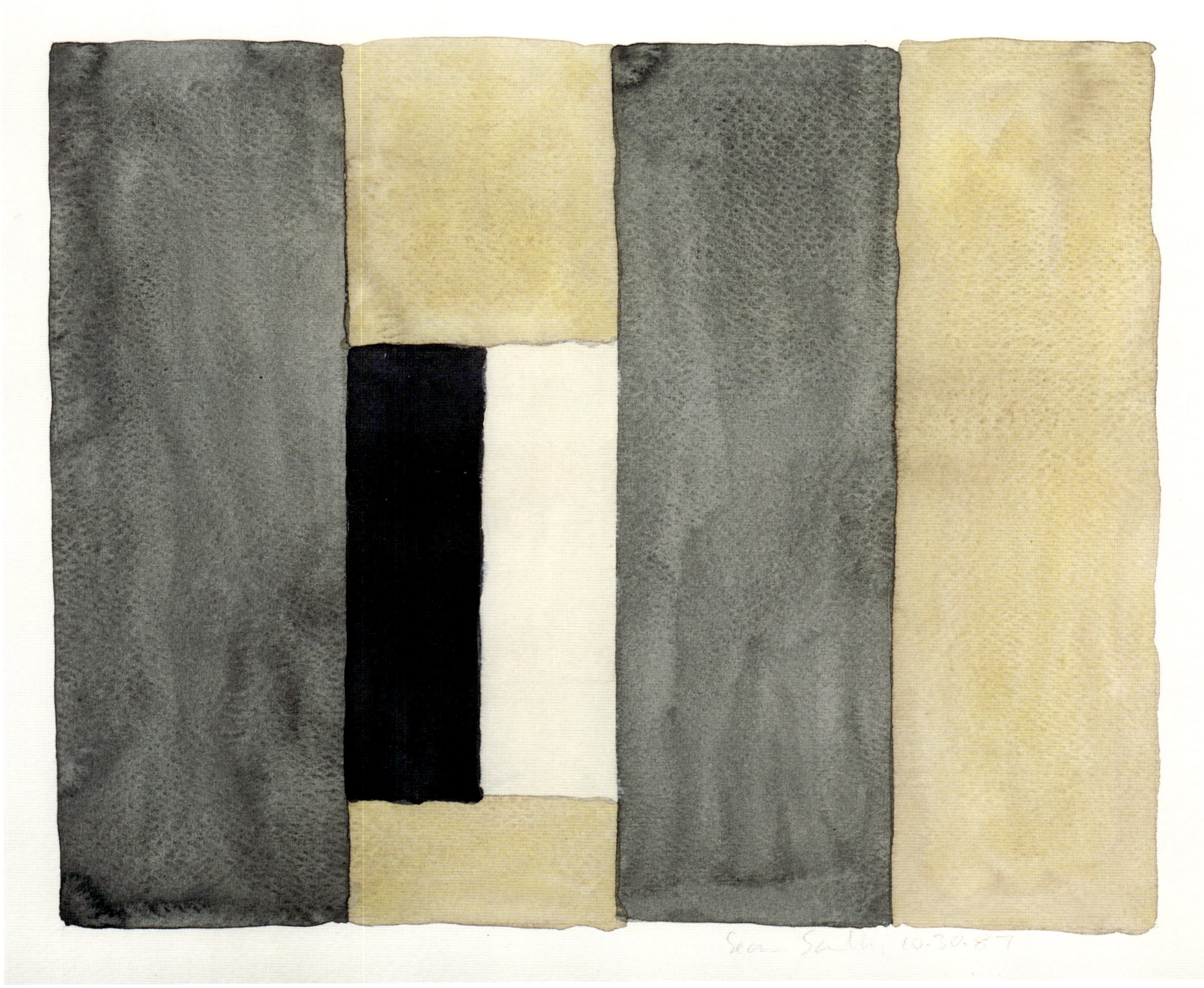

Cat. No. 20. *Untitled 10.30.87*, 1987

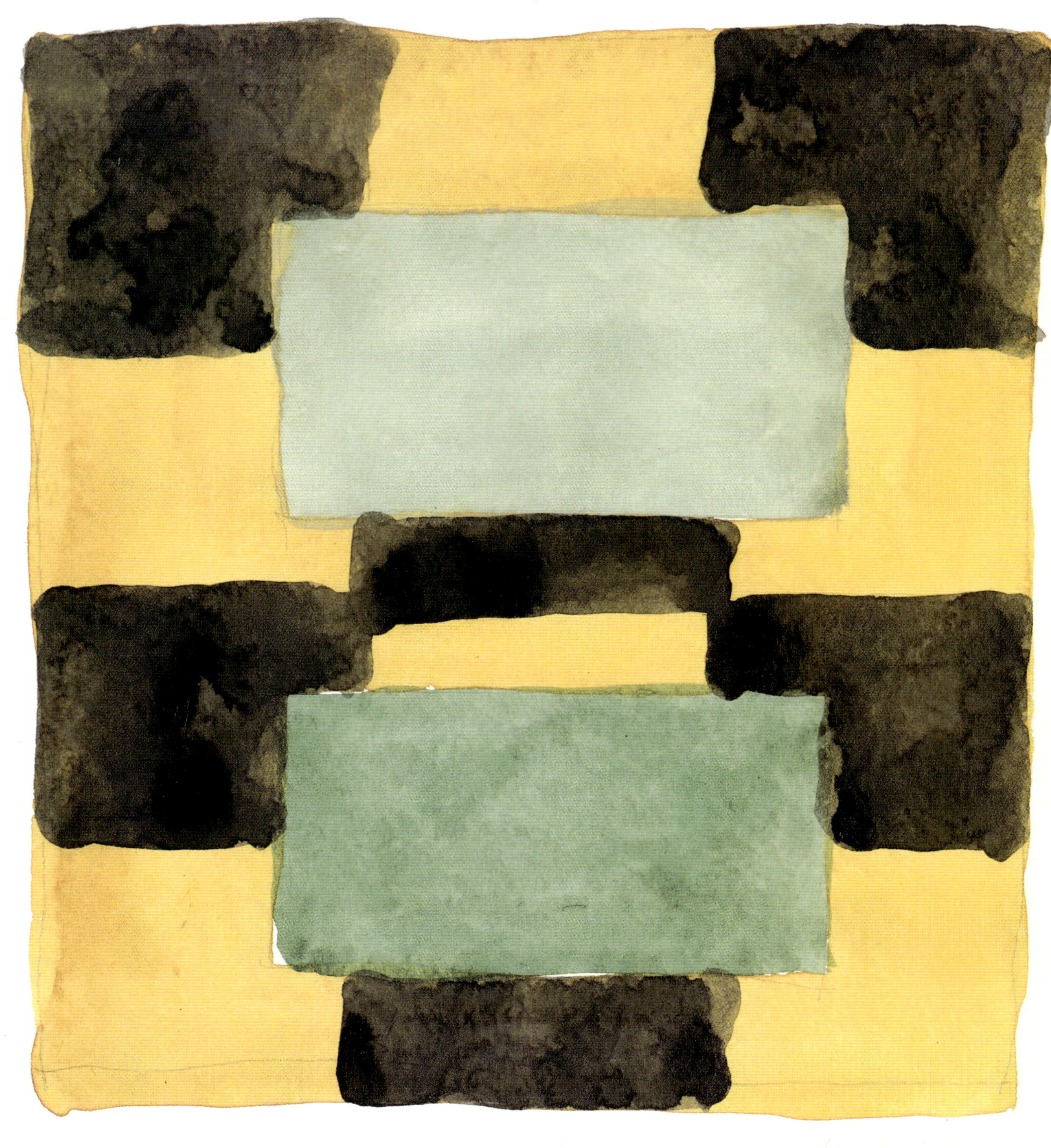

Cat. No. 29. *Untitled 11.13.91*, 1991

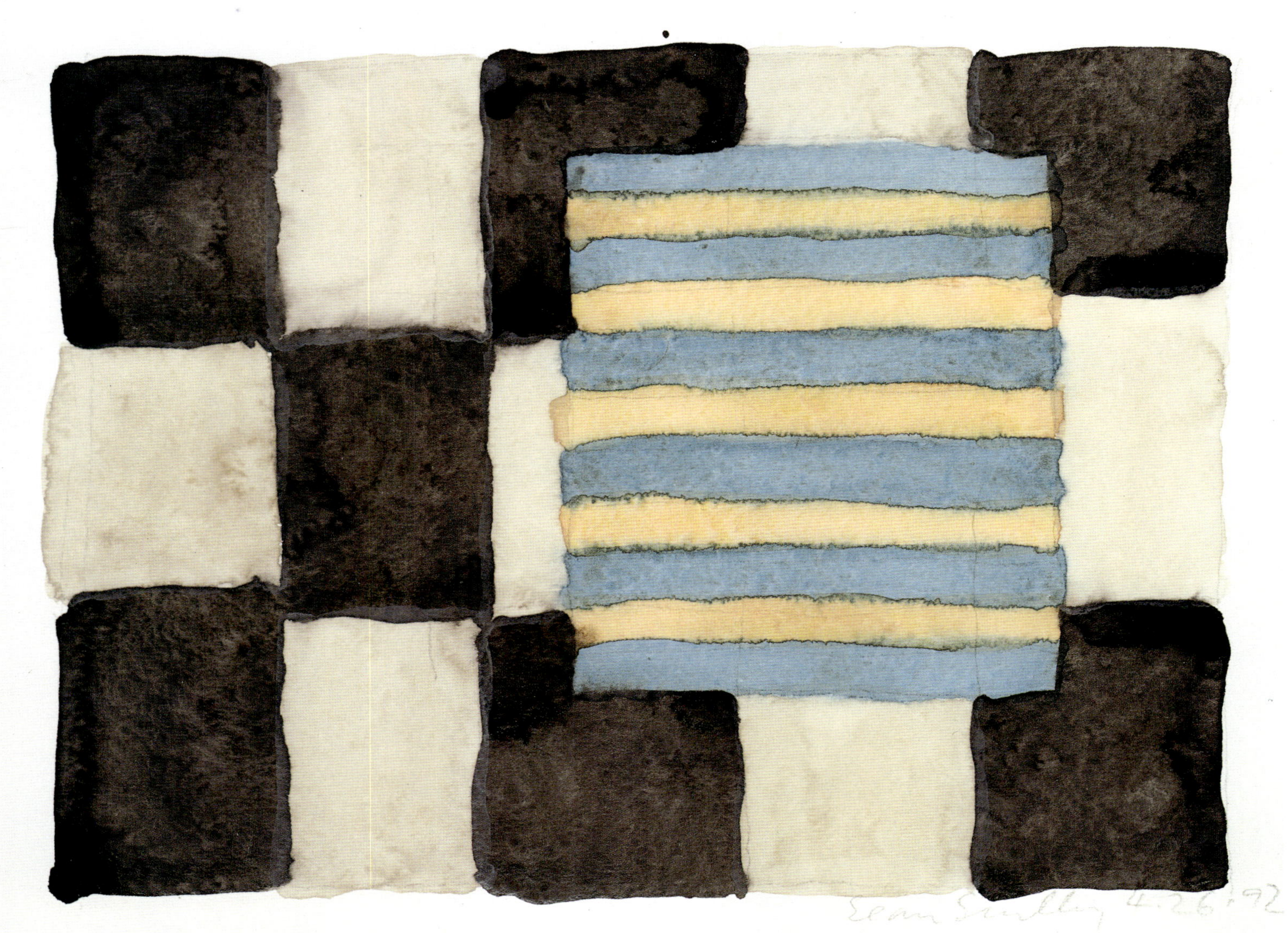

Cat. No. 32. *Untitled 4.26.92*, 1992

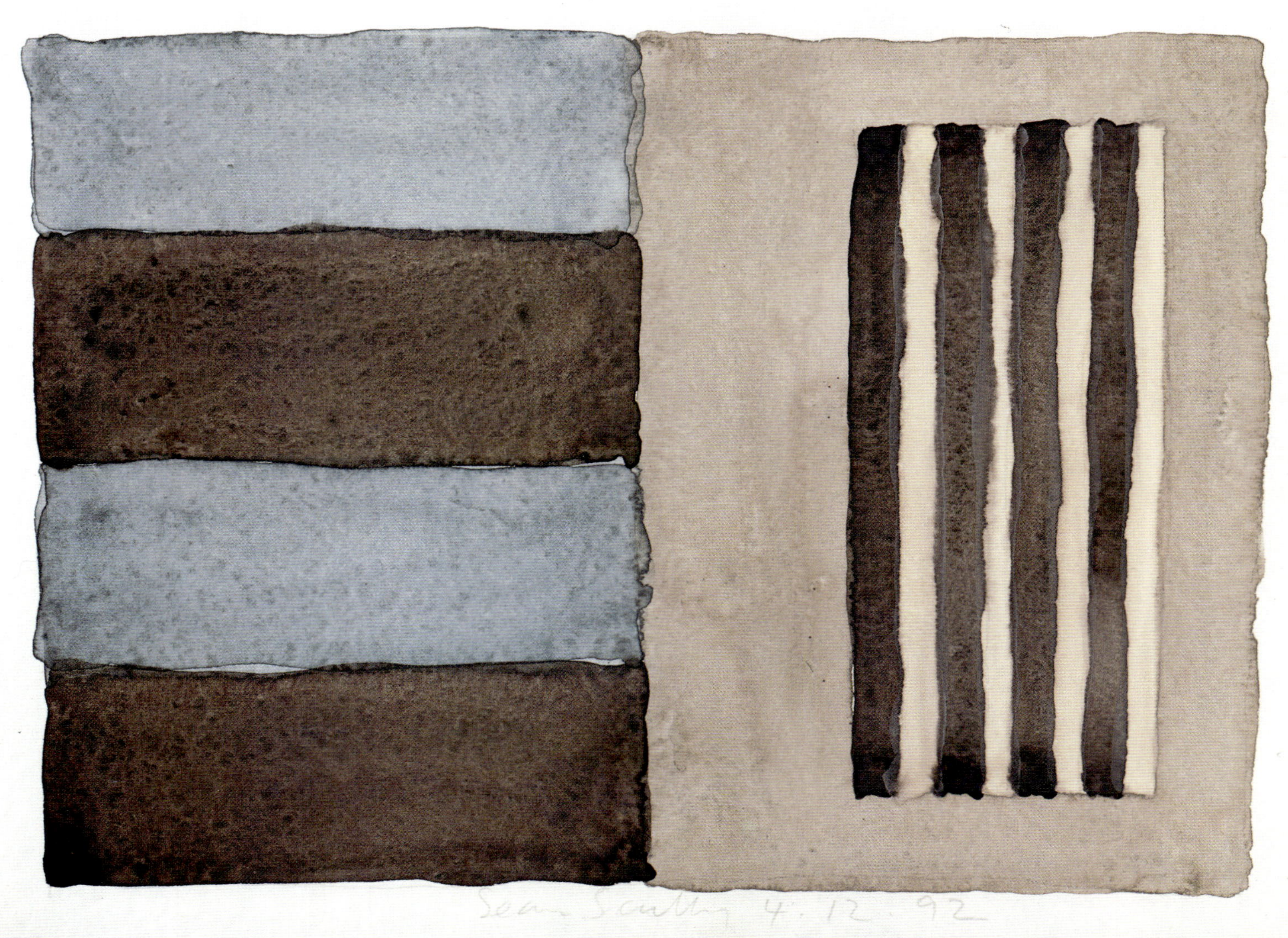

Cat. No. 31. *Untitled 4.12.92*, 1992

CHECKLIST OF THE EXHIBITION

THE CATHERINE PAINTINGS

1. *Catherine*, 1979
Oil on canvas
84 x 84 in. (213 x 213 cm.)

2. *Catherine*, 1980
Oil on canvas
84 x 35 1/2 in. (213 x 90 cm.) (two panels)

3. *Catherine*, 1981
Oil on canvas
96 x 108 1/4 in. (244 x 274 cm.)

4. *Catherine*, 1982
Oil on canvas
114 x 97 3/4 in. (290 x 246 cm.)

5. *Catherine*, 1983
Oil on canvas
115 x 96 in. (292 x 244 cm.) (two panels)

6. *Catherine*, 1984
Oil on canvas
102 x 134 in. (259 x 244 cm.) (three panels)

7. *Catherine*, 1985
Oil on canvas
98 1/2 x 99 1/4 in. (250 x 251 cm.) (two panels)

8. *Catherine*, 1986
Oil on canvas
96 x 130 in. (244 x 331 cm.) (three panels)

9. *Catherine*, 1987
Oil on canvas
96 x 120 in. (244 x 304 cm.) (two panels)

10. *Catherine*, 1988
Oil on canvas
100 x 120 in. (254 x 304 cm.) (two panels)

11. *Catherine*, 1989
Oil on canvas
102 x 136 in. (259 x 354 cm.) (two panels)

12. *Catherine*, 1990
Oil on canvas
108 x 60 in. (274 x 457 cm.) (three panels)

All works in the exhibition are from the collection of the artist.

13. *Catherine*, 1991
Oil on canvas
100 x 88 in. (254 x 223 cm.) (two panels)

14. *Catherine*, 1992
Oil on canvas and metal
84 x 120 in. (213 x 305 cm.) (two panels)

WATERCOLORS

1. *Mexico Maroata*, 1983
watercolor on paper
12 x 9 in. (30 x 23 cm.)

2. *Mexico Christmas Day 83*, 1983*
watercolor on paper
12 x 9 in. (30 x 23 cm.)

3. *Mexico Malloy*, 1983
watercolor on paper
9 x 12 in. (23 x 30 cm.)

4. *Untitled 3-12-84*, 1984
watercolor on paper
12 x 9 in. (30 x 23 cm.)

5. *Red Light 84*, 1984
watercolor on paper
10 x 14 in. (25 x 36 cm.)

6. *Untitled 7-30-86*, 1986
watercolor on paper
14 x 10 in. (36 x 25 cm.)

7. *Untitled 8-22-86*, 1986
watercolor on paper
14 x 10 in. (36 x 25 cm.)

8. *Untitled 8-22-86 #2*, 1986*
watercolor on paper
14 x 10 in. (36 x 25 cm.)

9. *Untitled 8-28-86*, 1986*
watercolor on paper
14 x 10 in. (36 x 25 cm.)

10. *Untitled 9-1-86*, 1986*
watercolor on paper
14 x 10 in. (36 x 25 cm.)

11. *Untitled 4-10-87*, 1987*
watercolor on paper
12 x 16 in. (30 x 41 cm.)

12. *Untitled 4-12-87*, 1987*
watercolor on paper
12 x 16 in. (30 x 41 cm.)

13. *Untitled 5-13-87*, 1987*
watercolor on paper
11 x 15 in. (28 x 38 cm.)

14. *Untitled 5-16-87*, 1987*
watercolor on paper
11 x 15 in. (28 x 38 cm.)

15. *Untitled 5-22-87*, 1987*
watercolor on paper
11 x 15 in. (28 x 38 cm.)

16. *Untitled 5-31-87*, 1987*
watercolor on paper
12 x 18 in. (30 x 46 cm.)

17. *Untitled 10-5-87*, 1987*
watercolor on paper
12 x 18 in. (30 x 46 cm.)

18. *Untitled 10-17-87*, 1987*
watercolor on paper
12 x 16 in. (30 x 41 cm.)

19. *Untitled 10-26-87*, 1987*
watercolor on paper
11 x 15 in. (28 x 38 cm.)

20. *Untitled 10-30-87*, 1987*
watercolor on paper
12 x 18 in. (30 x 46 cm.)

21. *Untitled 11-7-87*, 1987*
watercolor on paper
12 x 18 in. (30 x 46 cm.)

22. *Untitled 2-20-90*, 1990*
watercolor on paper
12 x 16 in. (30 x 41 cm.)

23. *Untitled 2-24-90*, 1990*
watercolor on paper
12 x 16 in. (30 x 41 cm.)

24. *Untitled 11-18-90*, 1990
watercolor on paper
15 x 18 in. (38 x 46 cm.)

25. *Untitled 1-6-91*, 1991
watercolor on paper
10 x 14 in. (25 x 36 cm.)

26. *Untitled 1-7-91*, 1991
watercolor on paper
10 x 14 in. (25 x 36 cm.)

27. *Untitled 1-9-91*, 1991
watercolor on paper
10 x 14 in. (25 x 36 cm.)

28. *Untitled 4-18-91*, 1991
watercolor on paper
10 x 14 in. (25 x 36 cm.)

29. *Untitled 11-13-91*, 1991
watercolor on paper
14 x 10 in. (36 x 25 cm.)

30. *Untitled 4-11-92*, 1992
watercolor on paper
15 x 18 in. (38 x 46 cm.)

31. *Untitled 4-12-92*, 1992
watercolor on paper
10 x 14 in. (25 x 36 cm.)

32. *Untitled 4-26-92*, 1992
watercolor on paper
10 x 14 in. (25 x 36 cm.)

SEAN SCULLY

1945	Born in Dublin, Ireland
1949	Family moves to London, England
1965-68	Croydon College of Art, London
1970	Receives Stuyvesant Foundation Prize
1968-72	Attends Newcastle University, England
1972-73	Harvard University, Cambridge, Massachusetts
1973-75	Taught at Chelsea School of Art and Goldsmiths' School of Art
1973	First one-man exhibition at the Rowan Gallery, London
1975	Moves to the United States
1977	First one-man exhibition in the United States at the Duffy-Gibbs Gallery, New York
1977-83	Taught at Princeton University, New Jersey
1981	Ten-year retrospective exhibition organized by the Ikon Gallery, Birmingham,England
1983	Receives Guggenheim Fellowship Becomes an American citizen
1984	Receives Artist's Fellowship from the National Endowment for the Arts
1985	First one-man exhibition in an American museum organized by the Carnegie Institute, Pittsburgh
1989-90	Major retrospective exhibition organized by the Whitechapel Art Gallery, London
1990	Monograph by Maurice Poirier published by Hudson Hills Press, New York

Lives in New York City and London

ONE MAN EXHIBITIONS

1993	Mary Boone Gallery, New York
1992	Waddington Galleries, London Daniel Weinberg Gallery, Santa Monica
1991	Jamileh Weber Gallery, Zurich
1990	Karsten Greve Gallery, Cologne Galerie de France, Paris David McKee Gallery, New York
1989-90	Grob Gallery, London
1989	David McKee Gallery, New York The Whitechapel Art Gallery, London, (traveled to Palacio de Velazquez, Madrid; Lenbachhaus, Munich)
1988	Art Institute of Chicago University Art Museum, University of California, Berkeley Fuji Television Gallery, Tokyo Crown Point Press, New York and San Francisco
1987	Pamela Auchincloss Gallery, Santa Barbara David McKee Gallery, New York

	Flanders Contemporary Art, Minneapolis
	Mayor Rowan Gallery, London
	Galerie Schmela, Dusseldorf, Germany
	University Art Museum, University of California, Berkeley
1986	David McKee Gallery, New York
1985	David McKee Gallery, New York
	Carnegie Institute, Pittsburgh, (exhibition traveled to the Museum of Fine Arts, Boston),
	Barbara Krakow Gallery, Boston, Massachusetts
	Galerie Schmela, Dusseldorf, Germany
1984	Juda Rowan Gallery, London
	Gallery S65, Aaslt, Belgium
1983	David McKee Gallery, New York
1982	William Beadleston Gallery, New York
1981	Rowan Gallery, London
	Museum fur Sub-Kultur, Berlin
	Ikon Gallery, Birmingham, England, (exhibition traveled through the United Kingdom under the auspice of the Arts Council of Great Britain)
1980	Susan Caldwell Gallery, New York
1979	Nadin Gallery, New York (special installation: Painting for One Place)
	The Clocktower, New York
	Rowan Gallery, London
1977	Duffy-Gibbs Gallery, New York
1976	Tortue Gallery, Santa Monica, California
1975	Rowan Gallery, London
	Tortue Gallery, Santa Monica, California
1973	Rowan Gallery, London

SELECTED GROUP EXHIBITIONS

1991	*Small Format Works on Paper*, John Berggruen Gallery, San Francisco, CA
1990	*Drawings: Joseph Beuys, Paul Rotterdam, Sean Scully*, Amold Herstand & Company, NY
	Anthony Ralph Gallery, NY
	Sean Scully/Donald Sultan: Abstraction/Representation, Stanford Art Gallery, Stanford University, CA
	Artists in the Abstract, Weatherspoon Art Gallery, University of North Carolina at Greensboro
	Geometric Abstraction, Marc Richards Gallery, Santa Monica, CA
1989	*The Elusive Surface*, The Albuquerque Museum, NM
	Drawings and Related Prints, Castelli Graphics, NY
	Essential Painting, Nelson Atkins Museum, Kansas City
	The 1980s: Prints from the Collection of Joshua P. Smith, National Gallery of Art, Washington, D.C.
1988	*17 Years at The Barn*, Rosa Esman Gallery, NY
	Works on Paper: Selections from The Garner Tullis Workshop, Pamela Auchincloss Gallery, NY

	New Additions, Crown Point Press, New York and San Francisco
	Sightings Drawing with Color, Pratt Institute, New York (traveling exhibition)
1987-88	*Logical Foundations*, Pfizer Inc., New York
	Works on Paper, Nina Freudenheim Gallery, Buffalo, NY
1987	*Corcoran Biennial*, Corcoran Gallery of Art, Washington, D.C.
	Harvey Quaytman and Sean Scully, Helsinki Festival, Finland
	Drawings from the 80s - Chatsworth Collaborations, Carnegie Mellon University Art Gallery, Pittsburgh
	Magic in the Minds Eye: Part II, Meadow Brook Art Gallery, Oakland University, Rochester, Ml
	Drawn Out, Kansas City Art Institute, MO
1986	*After Matisse*, traveling exhibition organized by Independent Curators, Inc.
	An American Renaissance in Art: Painting and Sculpture since 1940, Fort Lauderdale Museum of Fine Art, FL
	Public and Private: American Prints Today, Brooklyn Museum of Art, NY
	Sean Scully and Catherine Lee, Paul Cava Gallery, Philadelphia, PA
	Cal Collects 1, University Art Museum, University of California, Berkeley
	The Hero Sublime, Charles Cowles Gallery, NY
	Structure/Abstraction, Hill Gallery, Birmingham, Ml
	Courtesy David McKee, Pamela Auchincloss Gallery, NY
	Detroiters Collect: New Generation, Meadow Brook Art Gallery, Oakland University, Rochester, MI
	Recent Acquisitions, Contemporary Arts Center, Honolulu, HI
1985	*Painting 1985*, Pam Adler Gallery, NY
	Abstract Painting as Suface and Object, Hillwood Art Gallery, C W Post Center, Long Island University, Greenvale, NY
	An Invitational, Condeso/Lawler Gallery, curated by Tiffany Bell
	Decade of Visual Arts at Princeton Faculty 1975-85, Princeton University Museum of Art, NJ
	Abstraction/Issues, a three gallery show at Tibor de Nagy, Oscarsson Hood, and Sherry French Galleries, NY
	Art on Paper, Weatherspoon Art Gallery, University of North Carolina at Greensboro, NC
	Masterpieces of the Avant-Garde, Annely Juda Fine Art and Judy Rowan Gallery, London
1984	*An International Survey of Recent Painting and Sculpture*, Museum of Modern Art, NY
	Currents #6, Milwaukee Art Museum, Milwaukee, WI
	Small Works: New Abstract Paintings, Lafayette

College and Muhlenberg College, Allentown, PA
Hassam & Speicher Purchase Fund Exhibition,
American Academy of Arts and Letters, NY
1983   *American Abstract Artists*, national touring exhibition
Nocturne, Siegel Contemporary Art, NY
Contemporary Abstract Painting, Muhlenberg
College, Allentown, PA
1982   *Recent Aspects of All-Over*, curated by Theodore
Bonin, Harm Boukart Gallery, New York
Abstract Painting, Jersey City Museum, NJ, curated by
William Zimmer
1981   *Arabia Felix*, curated by William Zimmer, Art Galaxy
Gallery, NY
New Directions, curated by Sam Hunter, Sidney Janis
Gallery, NY
1979   *New Wave Painting*, The Clocktower, NY
Fourteen Painters, Lehman College, NY
First Exhibition, Toni Birkhead Gallery, Cincinnati,
OH
1978   *Certain Traditions*, traveling exhibition, Canada
1977   *Four Artists*, curated by Per Haubro Jensen, Nobe
Gallery, New York
Rowan Gallery, London
1976   Invitational, John Weber Gallery, NY
1975   Contemporary Art Society, Art Fair, London
1974   *International Biennial of Art*, Menton, France
British Painting, Hayward Gallery, London
1973   *La Peinture Anglaise Aujourd'hui*, Museum of
Modern Art, Paris
1972   *Critic's Choice*, Gulbenkian Gallery, Newcastle,
England
John Moore's Liverpool Exhibition 8 (prizewinner)

SELECTED BIBLIOGRAPHY

For extensive bibliographies, including exhibition reviews, see Maurice
Poirier, *Sean Scully*, New York, Hudson Hills Press, 1990, and *Sean
Scully: Prints from the Garner Tullis Workshop*, New York, Garner Tullis,
1991.

BOOKS AND EXHIBITION CATALOGUES

*La Peinture anglaise aujourd'hui. Paris: Musée d'Art Moderne de la Ville,
1973.* Essay by Edward Lucie-Smith.
Sean Scully: Paintings 1971-1981. Birmingham, England: Ikon Gallery,
1981. Essay by Joseph Masheck.
An International Survey of Recent Painting and Sculpture. New York:
Museum of Modern Art, 1984.
Sean Scully. Pittsburgh: Museum of Art, Carnegie Institute, 1985. Contri-
butions by John Caldwell, David Carrier, and Amy Lighthill.

Sean Scully. New York: David McKee Gallery, 1986. Conversation with
Joseph Masheck.

The Fortieth Biennial Exhibition of Contemporary American Painting.
Washington, DC: Corcoran Gallery of Art, 1987.

Harvey Quaytman and Sean Scully. Helsinki, Finland: Helsinki Festival,
1987. Interview with Mari Rantanen.

Sean Scully. Berkeley: Art Museum, University of California, 1987. Essay
by Constance Lewallen.

Sean Scully. Düsseldorf: Galerie Schmela, 1987. Essay by Susanne
Lambrecht.

Sean Scully. London: Mayor Rowan Gallery, 1987.

Sean Scully: Monotypes from the Garner Tullis Workshop. Santa Barbara:
Pamela Auchincloss Gallery, 1987.

Sean Scully. Chicago: Art Institute of Chicago, 1987-88. Essay by Neal
Benezra.

New York Studio Events: Sean Scully. New York: Independent Curators,
Inc., vol 3, no. 1, 1988.

Sean Scully. Tokyo: Fuji Television Gallery, 1988. Essays by Takashi
Nibuya and John Loughery; Interview by Kazu Kaido.

Sean Scully. New York: David Mckee Gallery, 1989.

Sean Scully. London: Whitechapel Art Gallery, 1989. Essay by Carter
Ratcliff.

Sean Scully. New York: Hudson Hills Press, 1990. Essay by Maurice
Poirier.

Sean Scully. Paris: Galerie de France, 1990.

Sean Scully. London: Waddington Galleries, 1992. Essay by Paul
Bonaventura.

SELECTED ARTICLES

Adams, Brooks. "The Stripe Strikes Back." *Art in America*, October 1985,
pp. 118-23.

Artner, Alan G. "Stripe Up the Band." *Chicago Tribune*, January 17, 1988.

Beaumont, Mary Rose. "Sean Scully." *Arts Review*, October 23, 1987, p.
726.

Bennett, Ian. "Sean Scully." *Flash Art*, January-February 1980, pp. 53-54.

———. "Sean Scully." *Flash Art*, Summer 1989, p. 157.

———. "Sean Scully." *Arts Review*, August 31, 1979, p. 453.

Berryman, Larry. "Abstraction of Opposites." *Arts Review*, December
1992, pp. 18-19.

Bonaventura, Paul. "Sean Scully: `Hay que ligar la abstraccion a la vida.`"
RS, October 1989, pp. 26-34.

———. "Interview with Sean Scully." Exhibition guide to *Sean
Scully: Paintings and Works on Paper 1982-88*. Whitechapel Art
Gallery, 1989.

Brenson, Michael. "Sean Scully." *New York Times*, February 8, 1985.

———. "True Believers Who Keep the Flame of Painting." *New York
Times*, June 7, 1987.

Burr, James. "Sean Scully at the Whitechapel." *Apollo*, June 1989, pp.
432-33.

Carrier, David. "Piet Mondrian and Sean Scully: Two Political Artists."
Art Journal, Spring, 1991, pp. 67-70.

———. "Spatial Relations." *Art International*, Autumn, 1989, pp. 81-
82.

Carty, Ciaran. "Sean Scully." *Irish Independent*, November 29, 1981.

Cooke, Lynne. "Sean Scully." *Galeries Magazine*, August/September 1989, pp. 60-63.

Cotter, Holland. "Sean Scully." *Flash Art*, April-May 1985, p. 40.

Chrichton, Fenella. "Sean Scully at the Rowan." *Art International*, June 15, 1975, p. 58.

Dannatt, Adrian. "Interview with Sean Scully." *Flash Art*, May/June 1992, pp. 103-105.

Decter, Joshua. "Sean Scully." *Arts Magazine*, December 1986, pp. 123-24.

Faure-Walker, James. "Sean Scully." *Studio International*, May-June 1975, pp. 238-39.

Feaver, William. "Sean Scully." *Art International*, November 1973, pp. 26, 27, 32, 75.

———. "Sean Scully—Point of View." *Vogue* (British edition), April 1, 1975.

———. "Sean Scully." *Artnews*, January 1978, p. 133.

Fisher, Susan. "Catherine Lee/Sean Scully." *New Art Examiner*, June 1986, p. 52.

Gold, Sharon. "Sean Scully." *Artforum*, Summer 1977, p. 69.

Griefen, John. "Sean Scully." *Arts Magazine*, February 1980, pp. 35-36.

Higgins, Judith. "Sean Scully and the Metamorphosis of the Stripe." *Artnews*, November 1985, pp. 104-12.

Hughes, Robert. "Earning His Stripes." *Time Magazine*, August 14, 1989, p. 47.

Hunter, Sam. "Sean Scully's Absolute Paintings." *Artforum*, November 1979, pp. 30-34.

Larson, Kay. "Sean Scully." *New York magazine*, October 3, 1983, p. 82.

Lewallen, Constance. "Interview with Sean Scully." *View*, vol. 5., no. 4, Fall 1988.

Madoff, Steven Henry. "Sean Scully at William Beadleston." *Art in America*, March 1983, p. 157.

———. "A New Generation of Abstract Painters." *Artnews*, November 1983, pp. 78-84.

Morgan, Robert C. "Physicality and Metaphor: the Paintings of Sean Scully." *Art Journal*, Spring 1991, pp. 64-66.

Oliver, Georgina. "Sean Scully." *Connoisseur*, December 1973, p. 302.

Poirier, Maurice. "Sean Scully." *Artnews*, January 1987, p. 160.

Ratcliff, Carter. "Artist's Dialogue: Sean Scully, A Language of Materials." *Architectural Digest*, February 1988, pp. 54, 62, 64B, 64D.

Raynor, Vivien. "Sean Scully." *New York Times*, June 19, 1987.

Russell, John. "Sean Scully." *New York Times*, December 10, 1976.

———. "Sean Scully." *New York Times*, March 4, 1977.

———. "Sean Scully." *New York Times*, December 14, 1979.

———. "Sean Scully." *New York Times*, January 23, 1981.

———. "Sean Scully." *New York Times*, December 24, 1982.

———. "Sean Scully." *New York Times*, October 20, 1986, p. 99.

Schappell, Elissa. "Sean Scully: Star of Stripes." *GQ* (British edition), April-May 1989, pp. 114-21.

Silverman, Andrea. "Sean Scully." *Artnews*, October 1986, pp. 98-99.